FABU

FABULOUS FISH

150 Healthful Recipes for Cooking Seafood

JOEL RAPP

Illustrations by
Paula Munck

Fawcett Columbine · New York

A Fawcett Columbine Book
Published by Ballantine Books

Copyright © 1991 by Joel Rapp
Illustrations copyright © 1991
by Paula Munck

Library of Congress Catalog
Card Number: 90-85051

ISBN: 0-449-90477-6

Text design by
Beth Tondreau Design
Cover design by James R. Harris
Cover illustration by Paula Munck

Manufactured in the
United States of America

First Edition: August 1991
10 9 8 7 6 5 4 3 2 1

Acknowledgments

Over the years, lots of good friends have sat at my dining table, and their glowing praise and empty plates have made cooking one of my greatest joys, no matter how many hours or how much work a particular meal has entailed. Their encouragement gave me the impetus to write this book, and I'd like to thank a few of them in particular: Paulette and Paul Noble, dear friends and real food people, who were always ready to come over and taste a new recipe and were never afraid to express their honest opinions; Sally and Marty Stone, who write great cookbooks, serve sensational meals, and introduced me to my wife; Ruth Katz, who can turn out a gourmet dinner on a hotplate; Anne Marie Huste, the best cook I know, who prepared a wedding feast for me and Susie that neither of us will ever forget; David Brod and Neil Rapp—the three of us have been breaking bread together through thick and thin for a long, long time; Lynn and Don Patterson, who probably have cooked more for me than I for them— lucky me!; Bernice and Howard Albrecht, my main tasters since my return to California; and of course, the three women in my life, Susie, Lisa, and Danielle. I love you all.

I would also like to thank all the people at Ballantine books for their continuing faith in me, with special thanks to my editor, Lynn Rosen, for shaping the book, and my eternal gratitude to Jane Mollman for her wonderful work editing the recipes.

Acknowledgments

vi

Contents

Introduction   1
    Health and Fish   3
    Basic Methods of Cooking Fish   11
    The Fish   15
    Substitutions   33
    The Recipes   35

*Appetizers, Soups,
and Stews*   39
    Appetizers   41
    Soups and Stews   56

Salads   73

Pasta and Rice   85
    Pasta   87
    Rice   93

Entrées   103
    Broiled or Grilled   105
    Poached, Simmered, or Stewed   131

Baked   170
Sautéed or Deep-fried   202

Sauces and Stocks   243

Epilogue   260

Index   261

Contents

viii

Introduction

ABOUT seven years ago, after fifteen years as a lacto-vegetarian, I decided to abandon the rigidity of that diet and add fish to my daily fare. There were many reasons. First and foremost, I was frankly bored with my regimen. And cooking vegetarian meals every night had become quite a time-consuming chore. I consulted with my doctor, I read everything there was to read on nutrition, and decided that adding a bit of salmon and swordfish now and then not only wouldn't hurt me, it might actually help. Fish, it turns out, is a very healthful and important food.

So I started collecting fish recipes and cooking fish in earnest. Soon, I had acquired dozens of fish cookbooks, many of them dating back to the 1930s; hundreds of fish recipes clipped from food magazines and newspapers, lots of recipes wheedled from chefs at fine restaurants, recipes from friends and relatives, and numerous concoctions I invented myself.

I began cooking fish every night I ate at home. I ordered fish when I ate out, then ran home to try to approximate those recipes. Some nights, when I had company for dinner, I'd prepare two, or even three, different types of fish and sauces. In short, I became obsessive. And in the bargain, a very good fish cook, if I do say so myself. My reputation began to spread, people began to invite themselves over for dinner, and the testing and tasting went on. I even entertained the notion of opening a restaurant.

Then one day, while fantasizing, I suddenly thought: Why not share my fish cookery—as I had my vegetarian cookery—with more people, in a book filled with delicious recipes? So I quickly wrote a proposal to my publisher, promising to deliver a fish cookbook that would satisfy the world's toughest critic—me. It would be, I hoped, the fish cookbook I couldn't find on any bookstore or library shelf—every recipe a treasure from the sea.

To compile this book, I set out to wade through my enormous collection of fish recipes and pick out the best to present to you in one practical and delicious package.

You won't find any pictures or text in this book about filleting fish, or killing lobsters, or boning skate—those disquisitions that take up so much space in so many other cookbooks—because, frankly, I don't cook that way and there's very little reason for you to cook that way, either. In almost every city of over 20,000 people there are at least three or four good fishmongers now, and most large supermarkets have a fresh fish section where the butcher will fillet your fish for you. And if you really would like to know how to fillet your own fish, I've never met a fishmonger or butcher who wouldn't happily show you how to do it.

I have supplied brief descriptions of the most readily available fish and how best to cook them, along with substitutions for each fish. You will also find information about the healthful aspects of eating fish, including a chart listing the number of calories, grams of fat, and milligrams of cholesterol for all the most common fish.

I'm sure you'll enjoy introducing more fish into your diet as much as I have. These recipes should help make it easy, healthy, and delicious. Bon appetit! (And à votre santé, too!)

Health and Fish

On June 16, 1989, I woke up at 5 A.M. with that mythical elephant sitting on my chest. I was bathed in a cold sweat, and the pain was nigh unbearable. In spite of the fact that I'd eaten way too much at dinner, I didn't have to be Dr. Salk to know this wasn't indigestion. Thirty minutes later, doctors at UCLA confirmed what I had guessed at once:

I was having a heart attack. An angiogram showed that an artery—but thank God, only one—was blocked due to atherosclerosis, a large accumulation of fatty deposits on the walls of an artery. They proceeded at once to perform angioplasty—a relatively simple (at least it looked simple to me, lying there watching it on a TV screen along with the doctors) procedure whereby a balloon is inserted into the clogged artery and inflated, thus opening the artery up and allowing blood to flow back into the heart.

Luckily the damage was minimal and I have gone back to living an even fuller and more active life than before. But the interesting thing was how surprised everybody was. "Joel, a heart attack? But that's impossible. He was a vegetarian for years, he doesn't eat meat, he's slim . . ." I was perplexed, too. I really thought I'd been taking good care of myself and maintaining a healthy diet. But then I realized that all the years I was a vegetarian (no meat, fish, or chicken), I was really a lacto-vegetarian, eating dairy products and eggs. Of course! All those omelets and cheese sauces and ice creams and cakes and butter had been just as devastating as if I'd eaten half a cow a day. My cholesterol count was a staggeringly high 290! (Anything over 200 is considered cause for concern, and I frankly hadn't checked mine in years.) My cardiologist advised that I eliminate as much fat and cholesterol from my diet as was humanly possible and go on a regimen of regular exercise. So I started walking two brisk miles every day, deleted all products with animal fat (except for an occasional little cheating), and watched my cholesterol go down to 180! For the last year I've eaten a diet composed of grains, vegetables, fruits, non-fat milk and fish. And fish, and more fish. And so should you.

Fish is full of protein, very low in fat, and very low (with the exception of shrimp) in cholesterol. In fact, fish is higher in protein than beef—19 percent versus 15 percent; lower in fat—5 percent versus as high as 30 percent; and filled with important vitamins and minerals, especially vitamins A and D. Fish is even slightly more healthful in the cholesterol and calorie categories than skinless chicken or white-meat turkey.

As important as the things fish *doesn't* contain is one thing fish does contain: Omega 3 fatty acids that will help to lower cholesterol and reduce the blood's tendency to form artery-clogging, heart-attack-inducing clots, and has also been found to help prevent certain cancers. Omega 3 is a polyunsaturated fat that's found in almost all fish, some varieties more than others. Generally speaking, the deeper the water the fish comes from, the more Omega 3. Fatty fishes such as salmon, trout, mackerel, bluefish, and tuna are among the best sources—even canned tuna has lots of Omega 3.

In fact, a recent study of 6,000 high-risk middle-aged men noted a *40 percent lower mortality rate among fish-eating Americans compared to the group that didn't eat fish.* A similar result was observed in a significant study published in 1989 in *The Lancet,* a prestigious British medical journal. It reported that of the nearly 2,000 men who had previously had a heart attack, those who were advised to eat at least two oil-rich fish meals per week had a 29 percent lower mortality rate over the next two years than those who were not advised to eat fish. The evidence is clear: Adding a few fish meals a week to a balanced diet can help keep the blood flowing through those narrow passageways to the heart. If I had known then what I know now . . .

WITH THE AMERICAN consumer's burgeoning awareness of the healthful and nutritious benefits of eating fish, fish consumption nationwide is up dramatically from ten years ago to about fifteen pounds per year per capita.* But last year there was a slight decline from the previous year's record high, caused by higher prices and public doubts about the wholesomeness of fish.

There have, indeed, been some problems with contaminated fish, but the National Fisheries Institute is taking giant steps to ensure more stringent controls that will eliminate the majority of the problems. For instance: Exotic fish, such as mahimahi, barracuda, and others im-

Los Angeles Times, June 15, 1989

ported from distant tropical and subtropical waters will be more closely inspected; medications and other chemicals used by some fish farmers to speed the growth of their fish will be more tightly monitored; methods of freezing fish at sea will be more carefully watched; and more attention will be directed toward where shellfish, such as oysters and clams, are harvested, using federal funds to check water conditions.

Public Voice for Food and Health Policy, a nonprofit organization working hand in hand with the USDA and the fishing industry, has issued several recommendations for avoiding potential problems when buying fish:

- Avoid seafood from contaminated waters. If you are catching your own fish, you should check with local health officials as to which areas are closed to sport or commercial fishing. Otherwise you must rely on a good fishmonger.
- Eat leaner varieties of fish, since contaminants are sometimes stored in fat. These fish include cod, halibut, pollock, shark, flounder, sole, snapper, sea bass, and haddock. You'll have to put your faith in your fishmonger when buying fattier varieties such as salmon, tuna, and mackerel.
- If buying whole fish, choose smaller and younger fish that have had less time to accumulate chemicals.

- Buy your fish *only* from a reputable fishmonger or supermarket. Stay away from "bargain" fish you might find at street markets or other outdoor vendors.

The most serious problems occur from eating raw fish, especially raw shellfish. It would probably be safest to stay away from all raw fish, but if you're a sushi lover like me and so many others today, then once again it's a matter of being very careful to select a sushi bar where the owners and chefs are as concerned about safety as you are, and closely inspect their fish—even using a magnifying glass on fish like salmon and tuna.

Yes, there are some legitimate fears when it comes to buying and eating fish, but the same can be said for beef, and poultry, and vegetables, and fruit. So select a first-class fishmonger, inspect and smell the fish you buy yourself, and then enjoy your fish dishes in good health.

NOW—LET'S DISCUSS the healthfulness of the recipes in this book with regard to calories, fat, sodium, and cholesterol.

Obviously, I am keenly aware of the need for healthy eating—for keeping fats and cholesterol to a minimum in your daily regimen. These recipes have been written to provide maximum gourmet pleasure, but any ingredient that contains more fat and cholesterol than your diet permits can be changed. Margarine or vegetable oil may be substituted for butter in any recipe—you may even spray your pan with a vegetable cooking spray such as Pam, if you like. Half-and-half may be substituted for cream, milk can be substituted in most instances, and even nonfat milk will suffice. And, of course, you can eliminate salt from every one of the recipes and barely miss it at all. Or, if you like the taste of salt and are on a low-sodium diet, use instead one of the salt substitutes available in your supermarket. I do feel, though, that unless you are on the very strictest of diets, you owe yourself the full glory of each recipe at least once.

As to the nutritional information about the individual fish, the chart that follows indicates the **number** of calories, **grams** of fat, and **milligrams** of cholesterol in a serving of approximately four ounces.

FISH	CALORIES	FAT (in grams)	CHOLESTEROL (in milligrams)
Albacore	177	7.6	70
Black sea bass	93	1.2	41
Bluefish	117	3.3	80
Clams (meat only)	80	.9	62
Cod	78	.3	65
Crab	93	2.5	108
Flounder	79	.8	60
Haddock	79	.1	68
Hake	100	.4	67
Halibut	100	1.2	62
Lobster (whole)	91	1.9	92
Mackerel	191	12.2	112
Mussels (meat only)	95	1.4	80
Oysters (meat only)	66	1.8	79
Salmon	220	13.4	80
Salmon (canned)	171	9.3	45
Salmon (smoked)	176	9.3	32
Scallops (bay and sea)	81	.2	33
Shad roe	130	2.3	68
Shrimp	91	.8	170
Skate	98	.7	N/A
Swordfish	118	4.0	39
Tilefish	79	.5	50
Trout	110	1.4	80
Tuna (raw)	145	4.1	38
Tuna (canned in oil, solid and liquids)	197	8.2	70
Tuna (canned in water, solid and liquids)	127	.8	70

Basic Methods of Cooking Fish

Fish can be broiled, grilled, baked, sautéed, deep-fried, steamed, or poached. You can also cook many kinds of fish in your microwave.

But no matter what method you choose, the most important factor in creating a great piece of fish is *cooking time.* A fish that's too rare must go back to the heat source for another cooking, a hassle that rarely produces good results, and fish that's overcooked is beyond salvation.

Luckily, there's a fail-safe method of determining the doneness of your fish. It's called the *Canadian Rule:* Allow ten minutes of cooking time for each one inch of thickness of the fish at its thickest part, no matter which cooking method you use. (This rule obviously does not apply to shellfish.) The Canadian Rule was conceived by the Department of Fisheries of Canada after long and arduous testing and is, for the most part, completely foolproof. For example: If your red snapper fillet or your swordfish steak is ½ inch thick, cook it for five minutes. If your halibut fillet or even your whole fish is two inches thick, cook it for twenty minutes. Over the years, this formula has proven fail-safe for me and almost every fish cook I know, and virtually guarantees that you won't commit the deadliest sin of fish cookery: overcooking your fish. I'll be repeating this warning against overcooking, because it really is the key to becoming a successful fish cook.

To test a fish for doneness, you may insert an instant-read meat thermometer into the thickest portion of the fish. Fish is ready to eat when the internal heat reaches 140 degrees. At 150 degrees the tissues begin to break down, allowing both juices and flavors to escape. If you have no thermometer, rely on your eye and your fork: The disappearance of translucence indicates that the fish is done, and if the flesh flakes readily when tested with a fork, you can be sure it's done. A good cook knows through experience how long to cook fish, but even the experts will watch the proceedings carefully to guard against overcooking. A final tip: when you begin cooking your fish, set a timer!

POACHING: Poaching a fish means immersing it in a cooking liquid and simmering the liquid until the fish is done. You can use a combination of half water, half white wine; plain water with a dash of salt; Court Bouillon (page 257); White Fish Stock (page 258); or any other liquid that will penetrate the fish and add flavor. Use the Canadian Rule to determine poaching time.

BROILING: To broil fish, season the fillets or fish steaks with lemon juice, salt and pepper if you wish, and a bit of garlic, perhaps. Lightly rub the fillets or steaks with a little olive oil and then set the fish in a greased broiling pan. Give your broiler at least fifteen minutes to preheat, then place the fish about six inches from the heat source. Use the Canadian Rule and turn once as you broil; each side of the fish should be just slightly brown.

SAUTÉING: To sauté or pan-fry a fish fillet or fish steak, heat two tablespoons of olive oil, vegetable oil, butter or margarine, or a combination of half butter and half oil, in a skillet, season your fish with lemon juice and salt and pepper, and any other herbs and spices you might want to use, and place the fish in the pan over medium-high heat. Follow the Canadian Rule, ten minutes per inch at the thickest part of the fish, turning with a slotted spatula once during the cooking.

BAKING: To bake fish, including whole fish, season your fish, place half a cup of water or wine or a combination of both or some other poaching liquid such as fish stock into a baking pan, place seasoned fish in pan, and bake in a preheated 425-degree-oven according to the Canadian Rule. If you're baking your fish covered with foil, allow an extra five minutes of cooking time.

GRILLING AND BARBECUING: If you're lucky enough to have a barbecue or grill, you'll get the advantage of that wonderful smoky taste that can only come from hickory or mesquite. To grill fish, season your fish with a marinade and oil the grill to prevent sticking. Then, when the coals are hot, hot, hot, cook the fish using the Canadian Rule, ten minutes per inch at the thickest part of the fish. The best fish to grill are those with the densest, thickest flesh: swordfish, tuna, shark, salmon, and halibut, for instance. Fish such as sea bass, sole, flounder, and other flakier fish will tend to fall apart on a barbecue or grill.

STEAMING: Steaming is an excellent method of cooking a delicate, lean fish if you want to retain its flavor and moisture. Steaming is similar to poaching except the fish is not actually immersed in the liquid. Instead, it is set on a steaming rack or colander at least two inches above boiling water in a large saucepan, kettle, or wok. The vessel is then covered tightly and the fish is steamed according the Canadian Rule. This is a particularly good method of preparing whole fish.

MICROWAVING: Many delicious dishes can be cooked in your microwave oven. I often substitute the microwave when the recipe calls for poaching or baking. I suggest you add a microwave cookbook to your collection, not only because its recipes will be attuned to microwave cooking, but also because you'll get a much better idea of cooking times necessary. (Obviously, when using the microwave oven, the Canadian Rule does not apply.) It's really a matter of some trial and error, but, for an example, when poaching a one-pound salmon fillet in the microwave, I usually cook it for about six minutes.

The Fish

I am not what you would call an avid fisherman, although some of the fondest memories of my life have to do with fishing trips, both deep-sea and fresh-water.

My father used to take me fishing a lot. My first actual fishing experience was at a small resort hotel in the San Fernando valley called the Sportsman's Lodge. They had an artificial lake there, which they kept stocked with big, hungry trout. The deal was that they gave you a fishing pole, some dough for bait, a basket (or creel) to store your fish, and then charged you a certain price for every trout you caught. They cleaned the fish and you took them home and pan-fried them. The problem with fishing at the Sportsman's Lodge was that these trout were practically trained to jump out of the lake and into your creel, and it usually didn't take more than a few minutes to catch half a dozen or so.

From there I graduated to real lake fishing, which was pretty boring, except that the occasional crappie or perch we caught really did taste better cooked over the campfire under the stars.

The next step up was deep-sea fishing, and that was lots of fun. Sometimes we would go out on the half-day boat from the Santa Monica pier in Los Angeles and come back with rockfish, ocean perch, sand dabs, even an occasional halibut. And then of course there was the all-day boat out of Malibu, where you could come back with twice as many of those kinds of fish. And for pure sport, what could be more fun than hooking up with a school of albacore or yellowtail in the waters down by San Diego or off Catalina Island?

I continued to go on the occasional fishing trip all through college and my twenties and thirties, but quite honestly, it's been years since I went fishing. The last time was on a chilly, rainy night off Sheepshead Bay in Brooklyn, where I caught two rather nice-sized bluefish and a whopper of a cold—and although I miss it, I'm not panting to do it, if you get my drift. I do my fishing now at my fish market, and although it's not quite as sporting, it gets the job done, and there's not a whole lot of laundry to do when I get home.

Fresh versus Frozen

Fresh fish is simply fish that isn't, and has not been, frozen. It has not necessarily just been caught. In trying to determine the freshness of whole fish, check that the fish is firm to the touch and has clear eyes and red gills. But the only way you can be positive that the "fresh" fish you are buying is really fresh, especially with fish fillets, is to be able to trust your fishmonger. And your nose. If there's any hint of a fishy smell, don't buy the fish. Remember, the freshest any fish is going to be is about twenty-four to forty-eight hours out of the water, unless you've caught it yourself, because it takes time to bring it to shore and then distribute it to the fishmongers.

Frozen fish is just as good as fresh in most instances, especially if it has been flash-frozen aboard the fishing boat, and it will keep for up to three months in your freezer. The main thing to remember is that once you've defrosted a piece of frozen fish, it is unwise to freeze it again. That greatly reduces the flavor and changes the texture of the fish. When the time comes to cook your frozen fish, there's no need to defrost it—just double the cooking time according to the Canadian Rule.

Now, here's a rundown of the most commonly available fish and shellfish and the very basic facts you should know about each. Some of these fish are more readily found fresh on the West Coast, some on the East Coast, but most are available fresh or frozen in all parts of the United States.

ABALONE. When I was a kid, we used to go diving for abalone off the shores of Santa Monica beach and Catalina Island, where these mollusks clung to rocks and had to be pried loose. The shells made great ashtrays, and the delicate-tasting meat, once pounded and tenderized, was delicious simply sautéed in butter and then spritzed with lemon. Now the abalone is an endangered species, and you won't find it at many fish stores. If you stumble across an abalone steak someplace, buy it and try it. Just remember to slice it extremely thin and make sure it's been tenderized.

BASS. There are lots of fish in the sea, and a great many of them are bass. Included in this large and very tasty family are the bass I used to catch when I was a kid, the bass that hide in the kelp beds off the Pacific coast. We used to go out in a dinghy, sometimes three or four of us, and fish for calico bass, and sand bass, and kelp bass, and we'd always bring home the limit—but catching them was a real adventure, because you spent most of your day reeling in seaweed. These fish are absolutely delicious broiled, grilled, or sautéed. Other popular varieties of bass you'll see are white sea bass, black sea bass, Chilean sea bass, and grouper. The meat of these bigger fish, while just as delicately flavored as the smaller varieties, has a coarser texture, and the fish are most often sold as thick fillets or steaks. Sea bass can be broiled, sautéed, or baked. Freshwater bass, perhaps the most popular being striped bass, abound in lakes all over the country and are very similar to their seagoing cousins. Delicate and flavorful, freshwater bass can be sautéed, broiled, or grilled.

BLUEFISH. I can tell you from my adventure off Sheepshead Bay that bluefish are a terrific fighting fish. The two I caught weighed about four pounds each, but both times I was convinced I'd hooked up with Moby Dick. Their flesh is dark in color and they're quite fatty, with a very distinctive, almost fishy taste. The key word here is *almost:* Because of their high oil content, bluefish *do* tend to get fishy if not eaten very fresh, so be sure and smell the fish before you buy. Bluefish are best broiled, grilled, or baked, and go best with acidic sauces such as lemon, lime, tomato, or mustard, which offset their oiliness.

CATFISH. For years and years many people avoided eating catfish because they didn't like the way they looked. I don't blame them—a whole catfish with its bewhiskered face is not a thing of beauty. But its meat is a joy forever. Over the last few years catfish have crept into favor—in great part due to the sudden popularity of Cajun cooking ignited by the ubiquitous media prescence of portly Cajun chef, Paul Prudhomme, and in some part because they're now most often sold as fillets, so we don't have to look at whole ones anymore. Catfish have really delicious mild-flavored, lean, moist, white to pink meat, and because they're commercially farmed now in ponds all over the country, catfish fillets are readily available everywhere. Catfish are delicious deep-fried, baked, poached, and in casserole dishes and stews.

CLAMS. There are basically two kinds of clams available in fish markets or supermarkets: hard-shell and soft-shell. Most hard-shell clams, such as littlenecks and cherry-stones, can be eaten raw, steamed, baked, cooked in a stew or in a sauce for pasta; larger hard-shell clams are used in chowder. Soft-shell clams are basically the clams we know as "steamers." In buying clams, put your faith in your fishmonger that the clams have not been harvested in tainted waters and that there are no cracked shells among them—these could be spoiled.

COD. It is said that "cod feeds the world." Actually, the right to fish for cod has been the cause of some very serious "codfish wars" in certain icy waters. Many boats have been sabotaged and sunk, and many lives lost in fights for fishing rights in territorial waters. In fact, the huge supply of cod in North Atlantic waters led to the colonization of New England. And the abundance of cod around Alaska, with its potential for a huge salt cod industry, was a contributing factor in its purchase by the United States. Cod has white flesh, is very lean, and has a very mild taste that is perfect for sautéing, broiling, poaching, or baking. Often marketed as "true cod," it's very inexpensive. Similar fish to cod include scrod (simply a cod that weighs under three pounds), haddock, hake, and pollock.

CRAB. A great delicacy that has soared to prices most of us can't afford. Yet the sweet, unique meat is so delicious that every once in a while I can't resist buying some crab, whether it be lump crabmeat, a whole crab or giant crab legs, or the delectable little soft-shell crabs (blue crabs that have just shed their shells). These are available during the summer and are best simply sautéed in butter (remember that the entire crab is edible). Universally available is a mock crabmeat, usually called "sea legs," which is a combination of pollock, seafood, and dyes. It looks like crabmeat and even tastes somewhat like crabmeat, but I prefer either the real thing or nothing at all.

FLOUNDER. Similar to sole, as are all flatfish, such as plaice, and, on the Pacific Coast, sand dabs. The most common varieties include petrale sole, gray sole, lemon sole, and Dover sole. All flounders have light, delicious, white flesh, although some varieties are thicker than others. Flounder (or sole) can be sautéed, baked, broiled, or poached in an endless number of ways.

GROUPER. See Bass

HADDOCK. A member of the cod family and very similar to cod in flavor and texture, but far more expensive because it's been almost fished out and because it's sweeter and tastier than cod. Haddock can be broiled, poached, sautéed, or baked, and is the basis of finnan haddie, haddock fillets that have been brined and smoked.

HALIBUT. I remember going out fishing on the half-day boat once, and almost being "skunked" (the term for catching no fish) until the skipper shouted "Lines up, we're going in!" I disconsolately started reeling in my line and felt this enormous weight on the end. I was sure I was pulling up a clump of seaweed, so imagine my surprise when I suddenly saw this huge halibut hanging on the end of my line. I don't remember exactly how big it was, but it won the jackpot for the biggest fish of the day on that boat. (I told you that story just for the halibut.) Halibut, a flatfish, is sold both as steaks and fillets, is firm, lean, and white, and is delicious broiled, grilled, baked, or poached and combines well with almost any sauce. Halibut fillets and steaks are thicker and the flesh is meatier and moister than that of other flounder-type flatfish. When cooked, halibut comes apart in little tiles, like sea bass, as opposed to flakes, like sole.

LOBSTER. How can anything as ugly as a lobster taste so good? Well, actually, the delicious sweet meat comes from the lobster's diet—he'll eat practically anything on the ocean floor that won't eat him, and his powerful digestive system gets rid of all the wastes. Again, as with crab, we're dealing with a luxury item when we talk about lobster, but what's life without an occasional indulgence? A couple of times in the last month my local fish market had beautiful lobster tails on sale, so I bought a bunch and we've been nursing them, pulling two from the freezer about once a week, letting them defrost, and then broiling them with a little butter and lemon juice. You can, of course, buy lobsters live, which is the best way, and then kill them either by immersing them in boiling water or stabbing them between the eyes. I'm not fond of killing things, but it seems easier on the cook to toss the lobster into the pot of boiling water. Lobsters can be steamed, boiled, baked, or broiled. When baking a lobster, allow about ten to twelve minutes per pound; when broiling, about eight minutes a pound, and when boiling or steaming, cook for anywhere from ten minutes up to a half an hour, depending on the weight. And don't forget to wear a bib when you eat a lobster. It's a dirty job, but somebody's got to do it!

MACKEREL. For many years I avoided mackerel at all costs—even free. Its strong, almost fishy taste was a bit too much for mine. But lately my tastes have changed, and I've been enjoying raw mackerel so much at sushi bars that I've cooked it a few times. Since it's so high in those Omega 3 oils that will help lower your cholesterol, I've decided to cook it even more. Mackerel flesh is dark and can be baked, broiled, or sautéed.

MAHIMAHI. Also called dolphinfish, mahimahi is *not* the mammal dolphin that is a member of the porpoise family. It's a delicious, dark-fleshed fish, native to Hawaii, that's a perfect substitute for swordfish and is best when broiled, grilled, or baked.

MONKFISH. Also known as "poor man's lobster" because of the amazing similarity in taste—sweet and mild—and texture, and the fact that it's less than half the price. If you've ever been in fancy French restaurants and seen lotte on the menu, they were offering you monkfish. You should buy only fresh, not frozen, monkfish; the flesh should have a pink cast, not completely white or, heaven forbid, gray. Monkfish is great in soups and stews, and can be broiled, poached, or grilled.

MUSSELS. Similar to clams, mussels are oval-shaped bivalve mollusks with blue-black shells. When I was a kid, my dad and brother and I would go surf-fishing early in the morning on the beach at Del Mar, just north of San Diego, where we spent some memorable summers. We'd buy a burlap bag full of mussels for a couple of dollars and use them as bait. Imagine my surprise when I discovered that they're not only tasty in their own right, but a true delicacy. Mussels taste very much like clams, sweeter even, are usually steamed, baked, or used in soups and stews, and can be substituted in any recipe that calls for clams.

ORANGE ROUGHY. This popular and delicious fish is caught off the coast of New Zealand and flash-frozen aboard the ships, so expect the orange roughy you see in the market to be labeled "fresh frozen." The pearly white flesh, with moist flakes and tender-firm texture, has a unique, crablike taste, somewhat similar to petrale sole. Orange roughy (my mother's favorite fish) can be poached, baked, broiled, or steamed.

OYSTERS. The old saw that you should only buy oysters in a month with an *R* in it is a good guide to getting succulent, fresh oysters, for they are at their best during the fall, winter, and early spring. There are many different kinds of oysters, all of them excellent. What I'd like to know is, who ever thought of opening one up and eating it? Oysters should be alive when you buy them—tap two oysters together and if they clunk as if they were rocks, they're alive. If there is a hollow sound, the oyster inside is probably dead. Raw oysters will keep up to a week in the refrigerator as long as they're unopened; once they're opened you should eat them at once if you're going to eat them raw. And don't wash them or you'll lose the valuable liquid inside which is called "liquor." The liquor should be clear; if it has a pinkish color, the oyster should be discarded. Oysters can be eaten raw, steamed, baked, or fried. If you're cooking oysters, don't cook them too long. As soon as the oyster starts to curl, it's done. The biggest reason many people don't buy oysters for home consumption is that opening them is a hassle. Ask your fishmonger to show you how.

POLLOCK. Another member of the cod family with tan or cream-colored flesh. It's cheaper than haddock or cod, with larger flakes, so it's especially good for soups and stews because it holds together very well. Pollock can also be served broiled or baked.

POMPANO. These small, flat, silvery fish are a real delicacy. They are usually sold whole and weigh anywhere from half a pound to three or four pounds. Pompano is not found in every market, but they are fairly prevalent on the East Coast. I've found the best way to cook pompano is to sauté or broil it.

RED SNAPPER. One of my favorite fish, and—good news—not too expensive. I buy nice, thick red snapper fillets, which are dark in color but turn white when you cook them. Snapper meat is lean and moist, and has a sweet, satisfying flavor. The fish can be cooked whole and stuffed, or the fillets can be baked, poached, broiled, or sautéed.

SALMON. Undoubtedly one of our most popular fish, the salmon has a truly unique flavor, different from all other fish. And of course its color—usually light orange or pinkish—is unique, too. Salmon can be served in myriad ways—whole, as steaks, or as fillets; smoked, broiled, grilled, poached, or baked. One of the more popular Northwestern varieties is called king salmon, which might just be a fitting title for the entire breed.

SAND DABS. See Flounder.

SCALLOPS. Scallops, both the small bay and the larger sea scallops, are immensely popular all over the country. Most scallop-lovers prefer their scallops unembellished by sauce, so they can savor the sweet, nutty taste. Scallops are perfect just sautéed in butter with a bit of garlic and lemon juice. They are also excellent grilled, broiled, poached, or baked. As with shrimp, don't overcook lest they become tough and rubbery.

SCROD. See Cod

SHAD AND SHAD ROE. Shad is a freshwater fish that is most abundant in February, March, April, and May. A member of the herring family, shad travel the rivers of the Atlantic coast between Labrador and Florida, and usually weigh between three and seven pounds. The meat of the female shad, fairly oily and cream colored, is tastier than that of the male, and is best broiled or grilled. But both male and female shad suffer from being too bony, which is why the shad eggs, or roe, is by far the most desirable element of this fish. Shad roe is sold in pairs and is at its most flavorful when the eggs are small and dark red. Fresh shad roe should be firm to the touch, not soft or mushy. Stay away from shad roe that's light, almost white, in color. These are eggs that have been taken just before spawning and will surely have a milder, less distinctive taste.

SHARK. I know, the conventional wisdom says that sharks eat people and not vice versa. But in the last couple of years most of us have discovered what connoisseurs have known for ages—that mako shark, thresher shark, and black tip shark all have meat that rivals the much more expensive swordfish for sweet flavor and firm texture. Sold only as steaks, which should have a slightly pinkish tinge, shark can be broiled, grilled, sautéed, or baked, and can be substituted in any recipe that calls for tuna or swordfish.

SHRIMP. Was it George Carlin who observed that it was odd something could be called a "jumbo shrimp"? Shrimp come in three basic sizes, small (bay), medium, and large, and can be bought either in the shell with the heads removed, or shelled and cooked. I don't think it's worth paying the extra price for cooked shrimp when you can very quickly shell and devein them yourself—simply remove the shell and legs and, with the point of a sharp knife, slit the back of the shrimp and remove the vein. It only takes a couple of minutes to cook shrimp. In fact, you should be very careful not to cook them any longer than that, whether they be broiled, poached, baked, or sautéed.

SKATE. Skate is just coming into its own on the seafood scene, especially on the East Coast, although it's harvested on both coasts. It's a member of the ray family and a cousin of the shark although it has a much softer texture than shark and many bones. Skate is purchased in "wings," each of which yields two edible pieces of fish. Be sure to buy it skinned and make certain it is very, very fresh. Skate spoils quickly—if you detect even a faint aroma of ammonia, pass it up. Skate flesh is lean, and ranges in color from pink to deep red. It can be baked, broiled, poached, or sautéed.

SOLE. See Flounder

SWORDFISH. Swordfish, because of its taste and texture, is known as "the steak of fish." Choose swordfish steaks with a pinkish tinge; stay away from those with lots of brown meat, or steaks that are pure white and dull looking. Swordfish steaks can be broiled or grilled, but be very, very careful not to overcook. Swordfish has a tendency to dry out quickly, and is better served slightly undercooked.

TILEFISH. Very colorful when taken from the water, tilefish has white, firm, lean flesh. This underrated fish, found mostly in East Coast fish markets, is delicious poached, broiled, or baked.

TROUT. Our old friend from the Sportsman's Lodge, trout is probably the most common freshwater fish commercially available because of its abundance in lakes and streams all over the country, and the fact that trout are fun to catch and great to eat. Trout, whether it be the rainbow, the speckled, the golden, or the brown variety (all varieties taste the same) has a delicate rich flavor and a firm, fatty flesh. This is one fish you might have to fillet yourself, but it's very easy to do, especially if you do it after the fish is cooked. As for the best way to cook trout, it really depends on the size of the fish. Little ones, from one half to one pound, can be broiled, pan-fried (sautéed), or poached. Medium-sized trout, from one to three pounds, whole or cut in fillets, should be broiled, baked, or sautéed. The big guys, from three pounds up, can be cooked whole, filleted, or cut into steaks, and should be poached, grilled, or baked plain or stuffed.

TUNA. This dark, almost red-fleshed fish only recently came out of the can and into the fish markets in the form of fresh, raw steaks. The three varieties most often seen are bluefin, yellowfin (ahi), and albacore. Tuna is very popular eaten raw as sushi, and can be delicious broiled or barbecued. But be *especially* careful not to overcook. In fact, just barely cook your tuna steaks so they're still almost raw and just warm inside. Any more than that and you might as well go back to the can.

Speaking of canned tuna—did you know it's America's most popular seafood, according to the National Fisheries Institute? (The rest of the top ten, in descending order, are shrimp, cod, pollock, flounder, clams, catfish, salmon, crabs, and scallops.) Canned tuna can be used to make tuna salad, tuna patties, tuna casseroles, or just eaten plain with a bit of salad dressing or vinegar. It is available as dark or light or white meat, and packed in either oil or water. The dark meat in oil is quite a bit less expensive than the white meat (albacore) in water, but as with anything else you buy, with canned tuna you get what you pay for. And please—be sure to buy only tuna that's "Dolphin safe"!

WHITEFISH (FRESHWATER). No relation to the ocean whitefish, this freshwater delicacy is most commonly sold smoked. Smoked whitefish can be bought whole or in chunks and is delicious as is, after you've removed the skin, of course. Small smoked whitefish are called chubs and can usually be found in Jewish delicatessens. Fresh whitefish fillets are usually marketed as Lake Superior whitefish, and can be broiled, grilled, steamed, poached, or baked. A succulent broiled whitefish fillet with a little lemon and garlic may just be the best fish of all.

WHITEFISH (OCEAN). Ocean whitefish is a warm-water fish that is very common along the Pacific Coast, especially near Santa Barbara. Ocean whitefish has a lean, mild-tasting meat, similar to bass. This is an excellent eating fish and can be broiled, grilled, steamed, poached, or baked.

Substitutions

In my headnotes to many of the recipes, I suggest that you can substitute other fish for the featured one, but here's a handy guide to substituting fish on your own, based on the density of the fish, the flakiness, the fatness or leanness, the firmness, and the taste.

THIN AND DELICATE FISH. This category basically includes all the flatfish: flounder, plaice, gray sole, English sole, petrale sole, rex sole, and, on the Pacific Coast, sand dabs. These fish are all interchangeable, and the best way to cook them is to poach, steam, or sauté. Lean fish retain their flavor best when their moistness is preserved, so it's wise not to expose them to the direct heat of grilling or broiling.

MEDIUM-DENSE, FLAKY FISH. This category can be divided into three subgroups: those fish that are lean and mild in flavor, fish that are mild in flavor but a bit oilier, and fish that are quite distinctive in flavor.

The lean and mild group, all interchangeable in any recipe, includes bass, catfish, cod and codlike fish such as haddock, hake, and pollock; small halibut, red snapper, and tilefish. These fish can be baked, broiled, sautéed, steamed, or poached.

The oilier group includes butterfish, black cod, Chilean sea bass (a truly delectable fish, one of my favorites), trout, and freshwater whitefish. Again, these fish are interchangeable in any recipe.

The distinctively flavored fish include bluefish, mackerel, pompano, and salmon. These fish are not interchangeable in recipes; use the particular fish specified. All of these fish can be grilled, smoked, broiled, sautéed, or poached.

MEDIUM-DENSE FISH WITH EXTRA FIRM FLAKES. These fish hold together extremely well and are excellent for broiling and grilling. They include small grouper, mahimahi, orange roughy, black sea bass, and blackfish.

DENSE AND MEATY FISH. These are the "steak" fish, those with thick, boneless flesh. They include large halibut, large grouper, shark, swordfish, and tuna. These fish steaks are best grilled or broiled but can also be quite delicious sautéed or baked. Because they tend to dry out very quickly in the cooking process, they should be marinated beforehand.

The Recipes

Okay, let's get cooking!

I have personally tested every recipe presented here at least twice—many of them several times—and what I have learned over the years about recipes and cooking in general is that no recipe is engraved in stone. Recipes are basically guidelines for putting together a variety of ingredients that marry well to produce a desired taste and texture. Not that you can't follow a recipe exactly and produce a fine dish. But the very nature of cooking is to experiment as you go along—add a bit of this, put in a little less of that. The best cooks, by and large, are people who love good food, who read about food, who aren't afraid to get into the kitchen and experiment. Becoming a great cook takes time and practice, but anybody, repeat anybody, can become a good cook if motivated to do so.

Some of the recipes in this book are more "difficult" than others, but what is a difficult recipe? It is one that requires more ingredients, more time to prepare, more concentration—in short, a recipe that carries a higher risk of failure due to human error than an "easy" one. But these recipes most often produce a more rewarding dish, so if you decide to take on a recipe that looks as if it might be tricky, make up your mind to really get into it—make sure you have the time to shop and prepare the dish. Don't put pressure on yourself or you're sure to goof up. Read the directions carefully, two or three times if necessary. Even though I've written these recipes so that almost every step is separately spelled out, you're still liable to miss something—leave out an ingredient, forget to cook or chop—unless you pay close attention.

Speaking of ingredients: Generally, the single biggest mistake you can make in cooking anything is to put too much of any one ingredient in. If a recipe calls for half a teaspoon of tarragon, for instance, and you put in half a tablespoon by mistake, it's going to be next to impossible to salvage the dish by adding and subtracting other ingredients. So I emphasize again: Read the recipe carefully, and once you know exactly how much of a certain spice or herb a recipe calls for, think for a minute and try to imagine the flavor. Does it seem to be too much for your particular taste? Then put in less, taste the result, and add more if you feel it needs it. You can't go wrong erring on the side of underseasoning, or putting in too little wine, or not enough butter, because you can always add more to taste. This is a cardinal rule of cooking. Memorize it.

And here's the most important thing of all: No matter how careful you are, no matter how hard you concentrate, no matter how attentive to seasoning and measurements you are when preparing the sauces in these recipes, it will all be for naught *if you overcook the fish!* The most perfectly executed sauce in the world is going to be wasted if the halibut or snapper or swordfish is tough and rubbery, the result of overcooking. Again, I beg you, try desperately to err on the side of undercooking because you can always put the fish back in the oven, or onto the grill, or into the skillet. Even though each recipe suggests a cooking time for the particular fish in that dish, I strongly urge you adhere to the famous Canadian Rule: Cook your fish ten minutes for each inch of thickness of the whole fish, steak, or fillet at the thickest part, no matter what method of cooking you're using.

Well, it's time we move into the kitchen and get to it.

Appetizers, Soups, and Stews

Appetizers

Escabeche

THIS DISH *is a fine hors d'oeuvre or appetizer. My friend Marty Stone brought the recipe back from Barcelona. You may use very small whole fish, such as anchovies, or fillets from halibut, tuna, or red snapper cut into ½-inch strips.*

**S E R V E S
6 T O 8**

2   pounds fish of choice (see sidebar)
    All-purpose flour
2   cups vegetable oil for deep-frying
    Salt and pepper
3   tablespoons olive oil
2   large garlic cloves, peeled
1   large carrot, scraped and thinly sliced
1   cup white wine vinegar
½   cup white wine
2   small jalapeño peppers
¼   teaspoon dried thyme
1   bay leaf
    Lettuce leaves, sliced black olives and sliced
        cucumbers

1. Dust the whole fish or fillets with flour.

2. In a deep skillet or wok, heat the vegetable oil over medium-high heat until it just begins to smoke, and then deep-fry the fish until golden. Remove fish with a slotted spoon and drain on paper towels. Season with salt and pepper to taste, place the fish in a large bowl, and set aside.

3. In another skillet heat the olive oil, add the garlic and carrot, and sauté for 2 to 3 minutes.

4. Lower the heat to medium, add the vinegar, wine, jalapeño peppers, thyme, and bay leaf and cook at a low boil for 10 minutes. Remove the bay leaf and discard.

5. Pour the marinade and vegetables over the fish and chill at least overnight and up to 2 weeks.

6. Serve on a bed of lettuce and garnish with black olives and cucumber slices. Serve cold or at room temperature.

Lobster Medallions with Avocado, Mango, and Basil Sauce

I SOMETIMES think I could eat lobster tails, hot or cold, every day and never get bored. Although they are delicious simply steamed or boiled with melted butter and lemon, try this recipe and I guarantee you'll remember it the rest of your life.

SERVES 6

THE SAUCE

2 tablespoons butter or margarine
½ cup chopped onion
½ cup White Fish Stock (page 258)
1 cup cream or half-and-half
1 cup firmly packed fresh basil leaves
  Salt and pepper

3 frozen rock lobster tails, ½ pound each, thawed
1 mango
1 avocado (preferably Haas)
  Fresh raspberries and dill sprigs for garnish

1. To make the sauce, melt the butter in a saucepan and sauté the onion over moderately low heat, stirring, until it is softened.

2. Add the stock, bring the mixture to a simmer, stirring, and simmer it for 5 minutes.

3. Add the cream and basil and simmer the mixture, stirring, for 2 minutes.

4. In a blender, blend the sauce until it is bright green.

5. Strain the mixture through a fine sieve into a bowl, season with salt and pepper to taste, and then chill the sauce, covered, for 2 hours.

6. Steam the lobster tails in a steamer over a pot of boiling water, covered, for 10 to 12 minutes.

7. Transfer the lobster tails to a cutting board and let them sit until cool enough to handle. Remove the meat from the shells and cut it crosswise into 18 medallions.

8. Peel the mango, cut the flesh from both sides of the pit, and slice it very thin, lengthwise.

9. Halve the avocado lengthwise, pit and peel it, and slice each half thin crosswise.

10. Spoon the basil sauce in 3 small pools on each of 6 plates, put a lobster medallion on each spot of sauce, and arrange a slice of avocado and a twisted slice of mango decoratively on each medallion.

11. Garnish each serving with 3 raspberries and a dill sprig. Serve chilled or at room temperature.

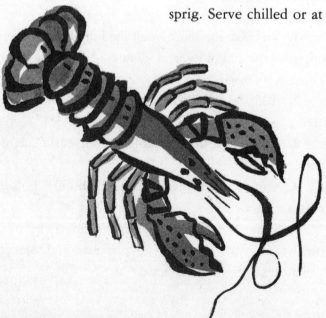

Seafood Sausage

FOR MANY *years I gave my friend Paul Noble a gourmet dinner on his birthday. One year I made this seafood sausage as an appetizer, and he hasn't stopped raving about it since.*

S E R V E S   8

2 pounds monkfish
1 pound cooked shrimp, shelled and deveined
½ teaspoon saffron threads
½ teaspoon white pepper
½ teaspoon nutmeg
½ teaspoon dried thyme
1 onion, peeled and chopped
1 tablespoon salt
1 tablespoon coriander seeds
8 tablespoons (1 stick) butter or margarine, cut into ½-inch pieces
1 cup breadcrumbs
  Lettuce leaves

1. In a blender or food processor fitted with the steel blade, purée 1 pound of the monkfish and ½ pound of the shrimp into a paste. Transfer to a bowl.

2. Purée the saffron, pepper, nutmeg, thyme, and onion and knead into the puréed fish.

3. Coarsley chop the remaining fish and shrimp and mix well with the fish purée, then add the salt and coriander seeds. Refrigerate for at least 1 hour.

4. Knead the butter and the breadcrumbs into the cold fish mixture.

5. Lay a large piece of plastic wrap on your counter and place the fish mixture on it. Shape the mixture into a large sausage shape, then wrap the plastic wrap around it and use it to roll and shape the mixture until it looks like a small salami. Twist the ends of the plastic wrap tightly and close them with twist ties.

6. In a large kettle, heat 6 cups of water to boiling, then add the fish sausage and boil for 10 to 12 minutes. Remove the sausage from the boiling water and refrigerate overnight.

7. When you are ready to serve, unwrap the fish sausage, which will be firm, and cut it into equal slices. Place a piece of lettuce on each serving plate, and top each with 1 or 2 slices of the fish sausage. Serve at room temperature.

Smoked Trout and Horseradish with Avocado

YOU CAN *find smoked trout in most gourmet food shops, delicatessens, and better fish markets. It's truly delicious just served plain, but this tasty appetizer takes full advantage of its delicate flavor.*

S E R V E S 4   T O   6

3   smoked trout (8 ounces each)
1½ tablespoons prepared white horseradish
      Juice of 2 lemons
½   cup sour cream
½   cup olive oil
      Salt and pepper
2   avocados (preferably Haas)
6   lemon wedges

1. Remove the heads and skin from the trout and discard. Pull the flesh carefully from the bones and flake it into a bowl, removing any remaining bones at the same time.

2. Add the horseradish, the juice of 1 lemon, and the sour cream, and mix well.

3. In a small bowl, whisk together the oil, the remaining lemon juice, and salt and pepper to taste.

4. Peel and slice the avocados lengthwise, divide them among individual plates, and pour some of the dressing over each portion.

5. Place portions of the smoked trout mixture alongside the avocados and serve with the lemon wedges at room temperature.

Clams on the Half Shell with Shallot-Wine Sauce

OFTEN LESS *is more—and this light, subtle sauce is just perfect as a complement to fat, juicy clams.*

SERVES 4

48

24 cherrystone or littleneck clams, scrubbed
3 cups dry white wine
8 shallots, peeled and finely chopped
   Salt and pepper
1 head Boston lettuce, rinsed, dried, and
    separated into leaves
2 tablespoons minced parsley

1. Scrub the clams thoroughly under cold water, discarding any that have cracked shells or that are not tightly shut. Open the clams over a bowl; catch the juice and reserve. Loosen each clam from both top and bottom shells, discard the top shell, and leave the clam in the bottom shell. Put the clams on a platter, cover with foil or plastic wrap, and refrigerate.

2. In a saucepan, combine the wine, shallots, and ½ cup of the reserved clam juice and cook over medium heat for about 45 minutes, until the liquid is reduced to about 1 cup. Season with salt and pepper to taste. Pour into a bowl and refrigerate for at least 1 hour.

3. Place the clams on a bed of Boston lettuce leaves and spoon a little sauce onto each clam. Sprinkle each clam with a pinch of parsley. Serve cold.

Sea Bass Seviche

SEVICHE IS *a cold, marinated raw fish dish that can be made with sea bass, snapper, or flounder, and served as an appetizer or first course. There are many variations on this theme, but this particular recipe is one of my favorites.*

**SERVES
4 TO 6**

1	pound sea bass fillets, cut into 1-inch pieces
1 ¼	cups fresh lime juice
1	cup minced yellow onion
1	cup minced red onion
3	scallions, minced
6	garlic cloves, peeled and minced
2	tablespoons minced fresh coriander
1	teaspoon Dijon-style mustard
1	tablespoon Tabasco sauce
1	teaspoon white wine vinegar
½	teaspoon salt
½	fresh jalapeño pepper, seeded and minced (wear rubber gloves)
	Freshly ground black pepper

1. In a glass or enamel bowl, combine the sea bass, lime juice, yellow and red onions, scallions, garlic, coriander, mustard, Tabasco, vinegar, salt, jalapeño pepper, and black pepper to taste and stir well.

2. Chill the seviche, covered with foil or plastic wrap, for at least 4 hours, preferably up to 12.

3. Transfer the seviche with a slotted spoon to chilled salad plates. Serve cold.

Tuna Caper Dip with Crudités

THIS THICK, *creamy dip is something between a tuna salad and a tuna tartare. Whatever, it's fabulous as a party-starter.*

S E R V E S 8

3   tablespoons vegetable oil
12 ounces tuna fillets, cut into 1-inch chunks
1   onion, peeled and sliced
1   onion, peeled and chopped
2   cloves garlic, peeled
2   tablespoons mild vinegar
2   tablespoons heavy cream or half-and-half
2   tablespoons mayonnaise
2   tablespoons capers, drained
½   cup sour cream
    Salt and pepper
    Crudités for dipping

1. In a skillet, heat the oil over medium-high heat and sauté the tuna for 3 minutes. Add the sliced onion and continue cooking for 2 more minutes, stirring and turning the tuna until the fish just flakes.

2. In a blender or food processor fitted with the steel blade, purée the tuna, cooked onion slices, raw chopped onion, garlic, vinegar, cream, mayonnaise, and capers.

3. Transfer the mixture to a bowl and stir in the sour cream. Season to taste with salt and pepper, then refrigerate until ready to serve as a dip with carrot sticks, scallions, radish roses, cauliflower and broccoli florets, and cherry tomatoes. Serve cold or at room temperature.

Tuna Tartare

SALMON MAY *be substituted for tuna in this delicious adaptation of steak tartare.*

S E R V E S   6

3 tablespoons olive oil
2 egg yolks*
6 tablespoons fresh lemon juice
2 teaspoons chopped fresh dill
2 teaspoons chopped fresh chives
2 teaspoons Dijon-style mustard
2 anchovy fillets, mashed to a paste
2 tablespoons minced red onion
2 teaspoons drained, minced capers
  Salt and pepper
1 pound tuna steak, chopped into 1-inch chunks
  and chilled
  Radicchio leaves or toast points as garnish

1. In a bowl, whisk together the oil, egg yolks, lemon juice, dill, chives, mustard, anchovy paste, onion, capers, and salt and pepper to taste.

2. Purée tuna steak in a blender or food processor just long enough for it to take on the consistency of chopped meat.

3. Add chopped tuna to the dressing and knead the mixture thoroughly. Serve chilled on radicchio leaves or toast points.

*Save and refrigerate the egg whites to make a delicious, cholesterol-free omelet.

Clams in Cream Sauce

AN EXTREMELY *elegant appetizer. Plan to spend some time on this one.*

S E R V E S   4

24	hard-shelled clams, scrubbed
2	shallots, peeled and minced
4	garlic cloves, peeled and minced
1½	cups dry white wine
2½	cups cream or half-and-half
1	tablespoon dry mustard
½	teaspoon butter or margarine, softened
½	teaspoon all-purpose flour
⅛	teaspoon celery salt
⅛	teaspoon cayenne pepper
⅛	teaspoon freshly ground black pepper
½	teaspoon soy sauce
¼	teaspoon Tabasco sauce
2	teaspoons minced fresh parsley leaves
¼	cup grated Parmesan cheese
4	parsley sprigs

1. Scrub the clams thoroughly under cold water, discarding any that have cracked shells or that are not tightly shut.

2. In a large saucepan, combine the clams, shallots, garlic, and wine and cook the mixture, covered, over high heat, shaking the pan, for 6 to 8 minutes.

3. As the clams open, transfer them with a slotted spoon to a plate, discarding the shells and any unopened clams. Set aside.

4. Bring the liquid to a boil over high heat and boil until it is reduced by half.

5. Add 2 cups of the cream and the mustard and boil the mixture until it is reduced to about 1 cup.

6. In a small bowl, knead together the butter and flour and stir into the cream sauce. Reduce the heat to low and cook the sauce, stirring, for 4 minutes.

7. In a chilled bowl beat the remaining ½ cup cream until it just holds soft peaks and fold it into the sauce, along with the celery salt, cayenne, black pepper, soy sauce, Tabasco, and minced parsley.

8. Stir in the reserved clams, divide the mixture among 4 greased shallow flameproof 1-cup baking dishes, and sprinkle the tops with the Parmesan.

9. Broil under a preheated broiler for about 1 minute, or until slightly browned.

10. Remove from oven and garnish each dish with a parsley sprig. Serve hot.

Warm Oysters with Orange Butter

TALK ABOUT *fine dining! This is a genuine ovation-getter—take a photo right before you serve and you may make the cover of a chic food magazine.*

S E R V E S   4

24	oysters
1	bunch watercress, stemmed and finely chopped
12	chicory or curly lettuce leaves, washed, dried and trimmed to about 3 ½ inches long
1 ½	cups fresh orange juice
1 ½	cups Beurre Blanc (page 246)
8	orange segments

1. Preheat the oven to 400 degrees.

2. Shuck the oysters and leave on the half shell, reserving the juices for another purpose. Set the oysters in one layer in a shallow baking pan, and place a teaspoon of watercress at one end of each oyster.

3. Arrange a few chicory leaves fanned out from the center of individual serving plates.

4. In a skillet, reduce the orange juice over medium-high heat until only ¼ cup remains. (The juice should be thick and syrupy.) Add the Beurre Blanc to the reduced orange juice and stir well.

5. Place the oysters in the preheated oven for 3 to 4 minutes, until they are warm and slightly puffed up.

6. Place 6 oysters on each serving plate and spoon orange butter on each oyster. Garnish each plate with 2 orange segments. Serve hot.

Trout with Apple Cream Sauce

LOOKING FOR an absolutely wonderful appetizer or brunch dish? Look no farther. All manner of fruit—especially apples—go very well with the distinctive taste of trout.

S E R V E S   4

1½   tablespoons butter or margarine
  4   rainbow trout fillets
  1   apple, peeled and sliced about ½" thick
  1   tablespoon chopped shallots
 ⅓   cup cream or half-and-half
 ¼   cup apple juice
 ¼   cup dry white wine
 ¼   teaspoon ground allspice
       Salt and pepper

1. In a skillet, melt 1 tablespoon of the butter over medium-high heat, add the trout fillets flesh side down and sauté until golden, about 2 minutes. Turn the fillets with a spatula and cook for another 2 minutes, or until they just flake.

2. Transfer the fillets to a serving platter, cover, and keep warm.

3. Add the remaining ½ tablespoon of butter or margarine to the skillet and sauté the apple slices until they are tender, about 3 minutes. Set them aside.

4. Add the shallots to the skillet and cook until tender, about 1 minute. Then add cream, apple juice, wine, and allspice and simmer the mixture until thickened.

5. Season to taste with salt and pepper, then return the apples to the skillet and heat through.

6. Pour sauce over the trout and serve hot.

Clam and Fennel Soup

THE SUBTLE, *licorice taste of fennel is a perfect complement to the unique flavor of the clam juice. And it's an exciting presentation, too.*

S E R V E S   4

2   tablespoons olive oil
1   large onion, peeled and minced
4   cloves garlic, peeled and minced
1   fennel bulb, trimmed, hard core removed, and cut lengthwise into thin strips, plus a second fennel bulb (see below)
3   tomatoes, peeled, seeded, and sliced into ¼-inch strips (or 8 canned peeled plum tomatoes, seeds removed, sliced into strips)
4   cups bottled clam juice
½   teaspoon freshly ground black pepper
    Pinch cayenne pepper
1   tablespoon tomato paste
20 littleneck clams, scrubbed
1   large fennel bulb, trimmed, seeded, hard core removed, boiled for 10 minutes

1. Scrub the clams thoroughly under cold water, discarding any that have cracked shells or that are not tightly shut.

2. In a large saucepan or soup kettle, heat the oil over medium heat and sauté the onion and garlic until they become soft and slightly brown.

3. Add the fennel strips and sauté for 2 minutes.

4. Add the tomato strips, clam juice, pepper, cayenne and tomato paste. Stir and bring to a boil.

5. Add the clams. As soon as they open, place the whole boiled fennel bulb into the center of a soup tureen and ladle the clams and soup around the fennel bulb.

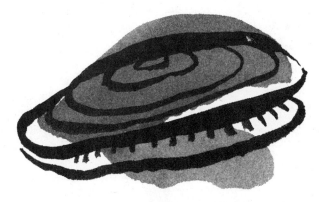

Appetizers, Soups, and Stews

Crab and Avocado Soup

WAY BACK *when, a crab and avocado appetizer with Russian dressing was about as chic and elegant a dish as you could order, right up there with lobster thermidor or tournedos of beef. Well there's still magic in the combined taste of these two great foods, and here it is in a silky cold soup.*

SERVES 4 TO 6

1 tablespoon butter or margarine
1 onion, minced
3 ripe Haas avocados
2 cups White Fish Stock (page 258)
   Grated zest of 1 lemon
3 tablespoons fresh lemon juice
½ cup cream
½ cup half-and-half
10 ounces crabmeat, picked over
   Salt and pepper
   Nutmeg

1. In a skillet, melt the butter over medium-high heat, add the onion, and cook, stirring occasionally, until the onion is just translucent, about 5 minutes. Remove from heat and reserve.

2. Peel and pit 2 of the avocados. Purée them in a blender or food processor fitted with the steel blade, then add the onions and purée again. Add the fish stock, lemon zest, lemon juice, cream, and half-and-half and purée until smooth. (Small bits of onion may remain in the purée.) Transfer the purée to a large bowl.

3. Stir the crabmeat into the purée, season with salt and pepper to taste, cover, and refrigerate for at least 2 hours.

Fabulous Fish

4. Just before serving, peel and pit the remaining avocado and cut it into ¼-inch cubes.

5. Divide the chilled soup among 6 small or 4 large bowls, and garnish with the avocado cubes and a pinch of nutmeg. Serve cold.

Lobster Bisque

I FIRST *discovered lobster bisque about thirty years ago—at a hamburger joint here in L.A., of all places—and it's been my favorite fish soup ever since. Here's a very elaborate recipe that has evolved from something I found in a magazine a few years ago and I assure you, is worth the time and the effort—a creamy, oceany essence fit for a king.*

S E R V E S 6

3   1¼-pound whole uncooked lobsters
6   tablespoons (¾ stick) butter or margarine
⅓   cup diced carrot
1   onion, peeled and diced
2   bay leaves, crumbled
½   teaspoon dried thyme
¼   cup Cognac
½   cup dry white wine
¾   cup bottled clam juice
1   tablespoon dry sherry
3   tablespoons all-purpose flour
1   tablespoon tomato paste
3   cups half-and-half, scalded
1   cup cream or half-and-half
    Watercress sprigs

1. Steam or boil lobsters, split them and crack claws, remove all meat from claws and tail, cut the meat into pieces, and reserve meat and shells in a bowl.

2. In a large sauté pan, melt 3 tablespoons of the butter, add the carrot and onion, and cook for 4 minutes, or until onion is soft.

3. Add the bay leaves, thyme, and lobster meat, then add 2 tablespoons of the Cognac and ignite. When the flame goes out, add the white wine, clam juice, and sherry. Simmer 15 minutes. Remove lobster from sauté pan and set aside.

4. Put shells (except for claws) and the contents of the sauté pan into a food processor fitted with the steel blade and purée.

5. In a clean sauté pan melt the remaining 3 tablespoons of butter, add flour, and whisk to make a roux. Cook for 2 minutes, whisking constantly, then add tomato paste and blend.

6. Pour in the scalded half-and-half, whisking until the sauce thickens.

7. In a soup kettle, combine puréed shell mixture and half-and-half sauce and simmer, covered, for 45 minutes.

8. Strain through a sieve to remove any shell particles, then return the mixture to the kettle, add the remaining 2 tablespoons of Cognac and the cream, and stir. Add lobster meat to briefly heat through.

9. Ladle into bowls and garnish each with a sprig of watercress. Serve hot.

Leek and Monkfish Soup

THE RICE *in this soup is an interesting touch, and monkfish, or lotte, seems almost perfect when cooked in this manner. This can be a wonderfully satisfying main dish when served with a rosemary-tinged sourdough bread.*

SERVES 6

7	cups White Fish Stock (page 258)
1¼	cups uncooked white or brown rice
4	large leeks, split, washed well, and cut into ½-inch-thick slices
2	pounds monkfish, cut into ½-inch cubes
2	onions, peeled and diced
½	teaspoon dried thyme
	Salt
⅛	teaspoon cayenne pepper

1. In a large saucepan or kettle, bring the stock to a boil and add the rice and leeks. Lower the heat, cover, and cook for 10 minutes.

2. Add the monkfish, onions, and thyme. Cover and continue cooking for 10 minutes more, or until the rice is tender and the fish just flakes.

3. Season to taste with salt and cayenne pepper and ladle into 6 soup bowls. Serve hot.

Creamy Scallop and Garlic Soup

THIS IS *another elegant soup that you can proudly serve as a starter course at your next fancy dinner party. Please be sure to put in enough garlic to give the soup a good, rich, garlicky tang.*

S E R V E S   6

20 large garlic cloves, peeled
6   cups White Fish Stock (page 258)
2   russet potatoes, peeled and cut into ½-inch cubes
2   cups cream or half-and-half
1   pound sea scallops, each halved crosswise
    Salt
3   tablespoons butter or margarine, cut into 6 pieces
    Cayenne pepper
    Several sprigs parsley, for garnish

1. In a large saucepan, cover the garlic cloves with 2 cups of the fish stock, bring the stock to a boil over medium-high heat, reduce heat to low, and cook the garlic, covered, about 10 minutes, or until it is soft.

2. Add the potatoes and cook, covered, until the potatoes are soft, about 10 to 12 minutes.

3. Pour the mixture into a blender or food processor fitted with the steel blade and purée until smooth.

4. Return the mixture to the saucepan, add the remaining 4 cups stock and the cream, and cook over medium heat, whisking frequently, until slightly thickened, about 8 minutes. Do not let the mixture boil.

5. Add the scallops to the soup and cook until they are translucent, about 3 minutes. Season with salt.

6. Ladle soup into 6 soup bowls, top each serving with a pat of butter, dust with cayenne, and garnish with parsley. Serve hot.

My Favorite Clam Chowder

MOST PEOPLE *have a problem remembering which type of clam chowder is red and which is white. Well, Manhattan is red and New England is white. Instead of giving you a mnemonic device to help you remember, I'll give you a delicious recipe that comes out pink, and will solve all your problems.*

S E R V E S   6

36 cherrystone clams, scrubbed
1 cup dry white wine
3 tablespoons butter or margarine
1 cup chopped onion
2 ribs celery, trimmed and chopped
2 teaspoons dried thyme
½ teaspoon dried marjoram
1 bay leaf, broken in half
⅛ teaspoon cayenne pepper, or to taste
¼ cup tomato paste
One 28-ounce can Italian plum tomatoes, with their juice
1 pound Idaho potatoes, cut into 1 ½-inch cubes
1 cup cream or half-and-half
¼ cup minced fresh parsley leaves

1. Thoroughly wash and scrub clams under cold water to remove any sand and grit, discarding any that have cracked shells or are not tightly shut. In a large pot, bring 2 cups of water and the wine to a boil and add the clams, bring the liquid back to a boil, then lower heat to a simmer and cook the clams until they open, about 5 minutes.

2. Transfer clams to a bowl and strain the juices through a fine sieve lined with 2 layers of paper towels to catch all shell particles and sand. Reserve this broth.

3. Remove clams from their shells and chop into bite-sized pieces. Set aside.

4. In a soup kettle, melt the butter and sauté the onion and celery until soft, about 4 minutes.

5. Add the thyme, marjoram, bay leaf, and cayenne, and mix well to combine.

6. Stir in the tomato paste and tomatoes, breaking up the tomatoes as you stir.

7. Add the reserved clam broth and bring the mixture to a boil, reduce the heat and simmer for 20 minutes.

8. Cook the potatoes in a separate pot of boiling water (or a microwave oven) until they are just done (firm, not soft).

9. Add the cream and the clams to the soup kettle and heat quickly (don't overdo this or the clams will toughen). Then stir in the potatoes and parsley. Serve piping hot.

Crab and
Corn
Chowder

I LOVE crab, and I love corn, and I love the fact that they marry very well. This is a nice soup to serve with a Chinese dish such as stir-fried vegetables.

SERVES 4 TO 6

½ pound fresh crabmeat, picked over
2 cups cooked corn kernels (frozen or fresh)
2 cups White Fish Stock (page 258)
4 tablespoons (½ stick) butter or margarine
½ cup sliced onion
¼ cup all-purpose flour
2 cups milk
⅛ teaspoon cayenne pepper, or to taste
Dash nutmeg
1 cup cream or half-and-half
Salt and pepper
Paprika

1. Flake crabmeat into a bowl.

2. In a blender or food processor fitted with the steel blade, blend corn kernels and ½ cup of the stock. Set aside.

3. In a soup pot, melt the butter over medium heat, add the onion, and sauté until soft. Stir in the flour and cook 1 minute.

4. In a separate pan, heat the remaining 1 ½ cups fish stock with the milk until just warm and add liquid to the onion mixture, stirring as you add.

5. Add the puréed corn and simmer for 10 minutes.

6. Stir in cayenne, nutmeg, and cream and bring to a simmer. Add crabmeat and season with salt and pepper to taste.

7. Ladle into individual bowls and sprinkle with paprika. Serve hot.

Shrimp-Celery Chowder

THE FISH *counter at my local supermarket has a rack where recipes are set out from time to time. I took this one from that rack (coincidentally buying a pound of shrimp, which just happened to be on sale), fooled with it a bit, and the third time around (after I'd added the potatoes) declared it engraved in stone. Try serving this with some warm cornbread for a near-perfect meal.*

1   cup chopped celery
1   cup diced potatoes
¼   cup chopped onion
2   tablespoons all-purpose flour
2   cups milk
16 medium shrimp, shelled and deveined
2   tablespoons butter or margarine
    Salt and pepper
    Parsley, for garnish

1. In a saucepan or soup kettle cook the celery, potatoes, and onion in 1 cup water (add more water to cover if necessary) until the vegetables are tender, about 10 minutes.

2. In a bowl, whisk the flour into the milk until it forms a paste, then add to vegetable mixture. Stir and cook over medium-high heat until soup thickens slightly.

3. Add the shrimp and cook for 2 minutes, then add the butter, stir until the butter is blended in, and season with salt and pepper to taste. Ladle into 4 soup bowls, putting 4 shrimp in each bowl, and garnish with parsley. Serve hot.

SERVES 4

Appetizers, Soups, and Stews

A Fine Kettle o' Fish

THERE ARE *endless variations possible with fish stews, bouillabaisses, and cioppinos. This recipe is really just a guideline to a rich, hearty fish stew. Feel free to improvise at your leisure. It'll be superb no matter what combinations of fish and vegetables you use. Just remember to serve it with lots of hot sourdough bread.*

S E R V E S   6

3 pounds (approximately 1 pound each) skinless and boneless monkfish, red snapper, and tilefish fillets.

3 cups White Fish Stock (page 258)

½ cup dry white wine

Salt and pepper

1 pound carrots, peeled, trimmed, and cut into julienne strips

1 teaspoon finely chopped garlic

⅛ teaspoon cayenne pepper, or to taste

½ cup finely chopped scallions

1 cup peeled, seeded, and diced tomatoes

1 pound cucumber, peeled, seeded, and cut into ¾-inch cubes

¼ cup fresh coriander leaves

Aioli (page 250)

1. Cut the fish into 1 ½-inch squares and set aside.

2. Pour the fish stock and wine into a large soup kettle, bring to a boil, and add the salt and pepper to taste, carrots, garlic, and cayenne. Simmer for 5 minutes, or until the carrots are tender, then add the scallions, tomatoes, cucumber, fish, and coriander. Cover and cook for 5 minutes.

3. Serve hot, garnished with dollops of aioli.

Monkfish and Shrimp Stew

HERE'S A *lovely seafood stew that's easy to prepare, perfect for a quick and hassle-free, cold-weather dinner.*

S E R V E S   4

1   pound monkfish
1   pound canned plum tomatoes, drained
3   tablespoons olive oil
2   teaspoons minced garlic
½   cup chopped onion
1   cup dry white wine
1   bay leaf
½   teaspoon minced jalapeño pepper (wear rubber gloves), or ½ teaspoon dried hot red pepper flakes
    Pepper
½   pound shrimp, shelled and deveined
2   tablespoons chopped fresh parsley leaves
    Cooked rice or couscous

1. Cut monkfish into 1-inch cubes and set aside.

2. Cut tomatoes into ½-inch cubes and set aside.

3. Heat oil in a heavy skillet and add garlic and onion. Cook, stirring frequently, until onion is opaque.

4. Add wine and cook for 1 minute. Then add tomatoes, bay leaf, jalapeño pepper, and pepper. Bring to a boil, cover, reduce heat, and simmer for about 5 minutes.

5. Add monkfish, stir, cook for 2 minutes, then add shrimp and cook entire mixture an additional 3 minutes.

6. Sprinkle with parsley and serve hot on a bed of rice or couscous.

Indonesian Tuna Stew

I ACTUALLY first sampled this dish in Indonesia, during a visit to Bali. Although it's always great, it's never again tasted quite as wonderful as it did the first time, when I sat on the dining patio of the Bali Hyatt Hotel, looking out at what surely must be the most beautiful setting in the world. Who says ambience isn't important for fine dining?

S E R V E S   4

3	tablespoons vegetable oil
4	thin slices peeled fresh gingerroot
4	garlic cloves, peeled and thinly sliced
Four	2-inch-long fresh hot red peppers, seeded and chopped
3	onions, peeled and cut into 1½-inch chunks
3	stalks celery, trimmed and cut diagonally into ¼-inch slices
8	scallions, halved lengthwise and cut into 3-inch lengths
4	tomatoes, cut into 1½-inch chunks
1	pound fresh tuna, cut into 1-inch pieces
1	cup unsweetened grated coconut
½	cup unsalted peanuts, lightly toasted
	Cooked rice as an accompaniment

1. In a large pot, heat the oil over moderately high heat and then add the gingerroot, garlic, and peppers. Cook, stirring, for 30 seconds.

2. Add the onion and cook the mixture, stirring constantly, for 2 minutes.

3. Add the celery and cook, stirring, for 3 minutes.

4. Add the scallions, tomatoes, and tuna and mix gently. Add 1 cup hot water and cook the stew, covered, for 3 minutes.

5. Garnish the stew with the coconut and peanuts and serve hot over the rice.

Catfish-
Potato Salad

*ARRANGED ON beds of
iceberg lettuce and
garnished with tomato
slices and quartered
hard-boiled eggs, this
makes a good luncheon
main course for four.*

**SERVES
6 TO 8
AS A FIRST COURSE**

2   pounds catfish fillets, sauteed and diced
3   cups potatoes, cooked and diced
1   tablespoon fresh lemon juice
3   tablespoons mayonnaise
1   tablespoon Dijon-style mustard
1   teaspoon salt
¼   cup minced scallions
2   tablespoons minced green pepper
½   cup peeled, seeded, and diced cucumber
⅓   cup finely diced celery

In a large bowl, combine all the ingredients and chill.
Serve cold.

Cooked Fish Salad with Carrots and Tomatoes

TO TURN this recipe into a main course for lunch, substitute a grilled 4- to 6-ounce piece of tuna, at room temperature, for the flaked fish on top of the salad.

SERVES 4

¼ cup olive oil
3 tablespoons fresh lemon juice
½ teaspoon Dijon-style mustard
  Salt and pepper
2 cloves garlic, peeled and minced
2 pounds poached, coarsely flaked fish such as salmon, cod, or sea bass
4 carrots, peeled and grated
1 tablespoon drained capers
2 scallions, trimmed and thinly sliced
1 tablespoon dried tarragon
4 plum tomatoes, cut crosswise into ½-inch-thick slices

1. In a bowl, whisk together the olive oil, lemon juice, mustard, and salt and pepper to taste. Add the garlic and mix well.

2. Put the fish in a glass or ceramic bowl, pour half the vinaigrette over the fish, mix thoroughly, then cover and refrigerate for 1 hour.

3. Just before serving the salad, place the carrots in a large serving bowl. Add the capers, scallions, and tarragon and toss. Pour on the remaining vinaigrette and toss until thoroughly mixed.

4. Mound the carrot mixture on a chilled serving platter and arrange the fish on top. Surround the salad with the sliced tomatoes and serve cold.

Salmon Niçoise

TUNA, CANNED or fresh, may be substituted for the salmon in this classic salad that is usually served as a main course, especially good at lunch.

SERVES 4

THE NIÇOISE DRESSING

3 tablespoons olive oil
½ teaspoon Dijon-style mustard
2 cloves garlic, peeled and minced
3 tablespoons lemon juice
¼ teaspoon dried basil, crumbled
6 anchovies, drained, rinsed, and mashed
   Pepper
1½ teaspoons chopped fresh parsley leaves
1 tablespoon capers, drained and rinsed

THE SALAD

1½ pounds cooked salmon, chilled
1 head red-leaf lettuce, washed, dried and separated into leaves.
1 pound cooked asparagus
1 pound cooked new potatoes, cut into ½-inch chunks
1 cup sliced carrots
2 ripe tomatoes, cut into wedges
One 6-ounce jar artichoke hearts, drained and halved
One 3¼-ounce can pitted black olives, drained
2 tablespoons grated Parmesan cheese

1. To make the dressing, combine in a bowl the olive oil, mustard, garlic, lemon juice, basil, anchovies, pepper, parsley, and capers and whisk until the mixture is emulsified. Cover and refrigerate for at least 1 hour.

2. Break the cooked salmon into chunks.

3. Line a serving platter with the lettuce leaves, place the salmon chunks in the center, and surround with vegetables.

4. Top with Niçoise dressing and Parmesan cheese. Serve cold or at room temperature.

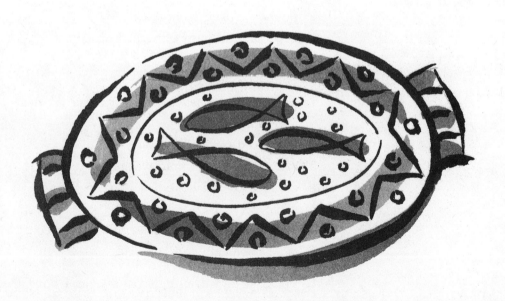

Shrimp Sunomono

(JAPANESE-STYLE SALAD)

WHENEVER *I see this on the menu at a Japanese restaurant, I order it. But it's much less expensive to make it at home—and you can whip it up in no time once you've refrigerated the dressing.*

S E R V E S   4

8 ounces cooked bay shrimp
½ cup white vinegar
1 tablespoon sesame oil
½ cup sugar
2 teaspoons salt
1 cucumber, peeled and thinly sliced
3 stalks celery, trimmed and sliced
2 scallions, minced

1. Rinse shrimp in cold water, pat dry with paper towels, and set aside.

2. In a bowl, combine the vinegar, sesame oil, sugar, and salt and mix well. Refrigerate for at least 1 hour.

3. In a salad bowl, combine the shrimp, cucumber, celery, and scallions.

4. Just before serving, pour the dressing over the shrimp and vegetable mixture and toss well. Serve cold or at room temperature.

Swordfish with Green Peppers

*A **SIMPLE** recipe that's deceptively delicious. Halibut steaks, cod steaks, or shark steaks may be substituted for the swordfish with no ill effect.*

S E R V E S   6

2   tablespoons olive oil
2   onions, peeled and coarsely chopped
2   garlic cloves, peeled and minced
2   tomatoes, seeded and chopped
2   pounds (about 5) green bell peppers, seeded, ribs removed, and sliced
    Salt and pepper
2   pounds swordfish steaks, cut into 1 ½-inch pieces

1. In a large skillet, heat the olive oil and sauté the onions and garlic over medium-low heat, stirring, until the onions are golden, about 3 to 4 minutes.

2. Add the tomatoes, the peppers, ⅓ cup water, and salt and pepper to taste, and cook the mixture over medium heat, stirring, for 10 minutes.

3. Add the swordfish and cook the mixture, covered, for 8 minutes.

4. Transfer the mixture to a platter and let it chill, covered, for 1 hour. Serve cold.

The Best Tuna Salad

TO CALL *any tuna salad "the best" takes a lot of nerve—but I've been experimenting with tuna salad for forty years and have eaten thousands of sandwiches. I've tried pickle relish, green peppers, red peppers, hard-boiled egg, celery, but in the long run, less is more. This recipe, basic as it is, will provide you with the ultimate flavor of tuna salad. The key: You must use solid white tuna packed in water.*

MAKES 8 BIG SANDWICHES OR 8 BIG HELPINGS ON A BED OF LETTUCE

Two 12½-ounce cans solid white tuna packed in water, drained
4 large scallions, green tops removed, chopped
1 tablespoon dried dill weed
3 tablespoons mayonnaise

1. In a large mixing bowl, chop the tuna until no big chunks remain.

2. Add the scallions and dill weed and combine the mixture.

3. Add the mayonnaise and stir with a wooden spoon until the mixture is thoroughly blended. Serve cold or at room temperature.

Tuna in Coconut Milk and Lime

THIS IS *an absolutely fantastic Tahitian dish that I first tasted in Hawaii. It makes a fabulous poolside lunch on a hot summer day—but don't be discouraged if you don't have a poolside. It's just as good in an apartment living room.*

S E R V E S   6

Coconut Milk

**M A K E S
A B O U T
1½ C U P S**

1 pound skinless, boneless tuna steak, cut into ½-inch pieces
⅔ cup fresh lime juice
1 cup coconut milk (see recipe below)
1 onion, peeled and finely chopped
2 tomatoes, peeled, seeded, and finely chopped
1 carrot, coarsely grated
1 cucumber, thinly sliced
¼ cup thinly sliced scallion greens
   Salt and pepper
3 hard-boiled eggs, halved

1. In a bowl, toss together the tuna and lime juice and let the tuna marinate, covered, for 15 minutes.

2. Stir in the coconut milk, onion, tomatoes, carrot, cucumber, scallion greens, and salt and pepper to taste.

3. Transfer the mixture to a platter and arrange the halved eggs around it. Serve at room temperature.

2 cups grated coconut

1. In a blender or food processor fitted with the steel blade, blend the coconut and 1¼ cups hot water for 1 or 2 minutes.

2. Let the mixture cool for 10 minutes and then strain it through a fine sieve into a bowl.

Pokee Tuna

THIS SALAD *is indigenous to Hawaii, where you find pokee salads made with everything from mussels to tuna to seaweed. And yes, the tuna is raw.*

S E R V E S   4

8	ounces bluefin or yellowfin tuna, cut into ½-inch cubes
One	2-inch-slice cucumber, peeled, seeded, and cut into ¼-inch cubes
3	scallions, trimmed and thinly sliced
2	cloves garlic, peeled and minced
¼	teaspoon dried hot pepper flakes, or to taste
1	tablespoon sesame oil
1	tablespoon soy sauce
3	cups (about 1½ bunches) spinach leaves, rinsed and dried
2	medium radishes, trimmed and thinly sliced
½	teaspoon toasted sesame seeds

1. Place the tuna in a bowl, add the cucumber and scallions, and mix. Sprinkle on the garlic and hot pepper flakes.

2. Sprinkle the sesame oil and soy sauce all over. Mix thoroughly, cover, and refrigerate for 2 hours.

3. Cut the spinach leaves into fine ribbons and arrange them on a serving plate.

4. Remove the tuna from the refrigerator and mix in the radishes, then mound the tuna mixture on top of the spinach. Sprinkle with sesame seeds and serve cold.

Pasta

Pasta with White Clam Sauce

GOT A *minute? Then try this absolutely magnificent recipe. There are simpler clam sauces, I'll admit, but none better. Serve with linguine or fettuccine, and be sure to sop up the succulent juices with big chunks of rosemary-olive bread.*

S E R V E S   6

2 pints minced clams (about 2 pounds)
3 tablespoons butter or margarine
3 tablespoons olive oil
6 cloves garlic, peeled and minced
1 cup chopped onion
Juice and grated rind of 1 lemon
½ teaspoon crushed red pepper flakes
1 teaspoon dried thyme
¼ teaspoon Tabasco sauce
1 bay leaf, crumbled
1 teaspoon dried sweet basil
1 teaspoon dried oregano
Pinch saffron
¼ cup all-purpose flour
4 cups bottled clam juice
1 cup plus 1 tablespoon dry white wine
1 tablespoon cornstarch
1½ pounds linguine or fettuccine, preferably fresh or imported dried
¼ cup chopped fresh parsley leaves
½ cup grated Parmesan cheese

1. In a saucepan, cook the clams until the juices are rendered. Drain the clams and discard the broth.

2. In another saucepan, heat the butter and oil over medium heat. Add the garlic and onion and sauté for 3 minutes, or until soft.

3. Add the lemon juice and rind, red pepper flakes, thyme, Tabasco, bay leaf, basil, oregano, and saffron. Stir to blend.

4. Add the flour to the mixture and blend well.

5. In a separate large saucepan, heat the clam juice and 1 cup of wine to a simmer. Add the garlic and onion mixture a cup at a time, stirring constantly. Simmer for 30 minutes over low heat, uncovered.

6. Combine cornstarch and the remaining 1 tablespoon wine and add it to the sauce, whisking until it is thickened.

7. In a big pot of vigorously boiling salted water, cook the pasta until al dente and drain thoroughly.

8. Meanwhile add the cooked clams to the sauce, and heat through.

9. Remove sauce from heat, add parsley and Parmesan cheese, and stir to blend. Serve hot over the freshly cooked pasta.

Monkfish with Pasta in Fresh Tomato Sauce

THIS IS *another good example of how best to use monkfish, which, although good on its own, becomes better when blended with other ingredients.*

S E R V E S   4

2 pounds monkfish
¼ cup olive oil
1 cup chopped onion
1 tablespoon minced garlic
4 tomatoes, peeled, seeded, and chopped
¼ cup dry red wine
1 tablespoon tomato paste
Salt and pepper
1 pound spaghetti or linguine
Chopped fresh basil

1. Cut the monkfish into 12 pieces and set aside.

2. In a large skillet, heat the oil over medium heat, add the onion and garlic, and sauté until the onion is soft, about 3 minutes.

3. Add the tomatoes, stir, and cook 4 minutes.

4. Stir in the red wine and tomato paste and simmer for 10 minutes.

5. Add the monkfish pieces to the mixture, cover, and cook for 3 or 4 minutes. Turn the fish over and cook another 3 or 4 minutes, or until the fish is cooked through. Season to taste with salt and pepper. Keep warm.

6. Cook the pasta in plenty of boiling salted water until it is al dente. Drain.

7. Serve the hot monkfish sauce over the cooked pasta, garnished with chopped basil.

Noodles and Smoked Salmon with Dill Sauce

THE SECRET to success here is making sure the smoked salmon strips are not cut too small—it's important to get the full, smoky taste of the salmon along with the dill.

SERVES 4 AS A FIRST COURSE

3 tablespoons minced shallot
½ cup dry white wine
1 cup cream or half-and-half
6 ounces dried egg noodles or ½ pound fresh
2 tablespoons snipped fresh dill
¼ teaspoon dry dill weed
¼ pound thinly sliced smoked salmon, cut into
     2-inch strips
   Salt and pepper

1. In a saucepan, combine the shallot and the wine and bring to a boil over medium-high heat, then reduce the heat and simmer until the liquid is reduced to about 2 tablespoons.

2. Stir in the cream, bring the mixture to a boil, and simmer for 5 minutes.

3. In a kettle of boiling salted water cook the noodles, stirring occasionally, about 3 minutes for fresh pasta and about 8 minutes for dried. Drain the pasta and transfer it to a large bowl.

4. Bring the sauce back to a boil, remove it at once from the heat, and stir in the dill and the dill weed.

5. Pour the sauce over the noodles and toss. With a large fork, stir in the salmon and season with salt and pepper to taste. Serve hot.

Squid-Ink Pasta with Scallops and Red Peppers

SQUID-INK PASTA, *which is black and has a most distinctive flavor, is just one of many new specialty pastas available in gourmet food stores and better markets. Another of my favorites is lemon and pepper pasta, delicious when served with sautéed or broiled swordfish chunks and a light oil and garlic dressing. Any pasta can be used in this recipe, but I like this particular color combination.*

SERVES 4

12   tablespoons (1½ sticks) butter or margarine
2   red bell peppers, seeded, ribs removed and cut into ½-inch slices
1   pound bay or sea scallops
½   cup dry white wine
2   tablespoons chopped fresh thyme leaves or 1 teaspoon dried
    Salt and pepper
1   lb. squid-ink pasta

1. In a skillet, heat 2 tablespoons of the butter. Add the red pepper slices and sauté them until they are tender.

2. Add the scallops and sauté the mixture for about 1 minute, until the scallops are just heated through.

3. Transfer the scallops and peppers to a plate and set aside. Add the wine to the skillet, and bring to a boil. Cook until the liquid is reduced by half.

4. Reduce heat to low and whisk in the remaining butter. Return the scallops and peppers to the skillet, add the thyme, and season with salt and pepper to taste. Set aside.

5. Cook the pasta in plenty of boiling salted water until it is al dente. Drain and rinse under hot water.

6. Combine the pasta and the scallop mixture, tossing gently to mix, then divide it among 4 plates and serve hot.

Pesto Pasta with Broccoli and Tuna

HERE'S A *very healthy and hassle-free pasta recipe that makes a lovely main course for lunch or dinner on a hot summer day.*

S E R V E S   6

1   pound rigatoni, penne, or ziti
4   tablespoons olive oil
4   cups broccoli, cut into bite-sized pieces
1   teaspoon minced garlic
   Salt and pepper
4   tablespoons Pesto Sauce (page 251)
1   cup scallions, thinly sliced
Two 9-ounce cans solid white tuna, packed in water
2   large, ripe tomatoes, cut into bite-sized chunks
12 black olives, pitted and sliced
2   tablespoons chopped fresh cilantro or parsley leaves
   Thinly sliced scallions for garnish

1. In a pot of boiling salted water, cook the pasta until it is al dente. Drain, add 2 tablespoons of olive oil, toss, and set aside to cool in a large mixing bowl.

2. In another pot of boiling water, steam or boil the broccoli until it's barely cooked.

3. In a large skillet, heat the remaining 2 tablespoons olive oil, then add the broccoli, garlic, salt and pepper to taste. Cook over medium heat until the broccoli is tender.

4. Add the broccoli mixture to the pasta and toss, then add the pesto sauce and mix well. Add 1 cup of scallions, tuna, tomatoes, and olives and toss again. Add the cilantro or parsley, garnish with the sliced scallions and serve at room temperature.

Rice

Haddock in Jalapeño-Peanut Sauce

ON A RECENT *trip to Singapore, I asked a friend who lived there where the locals ate. He sent me to a small diner right around the corner from one of the huge, chichi hotels. Here I first experienced what hot food was really about—people shoveling white rice in their mouths to put out the flames after every bite of sauce-covered fish, or beef, or chicken. You can adjust the heat of this recipe by adding more or less jalapeño, to taste.*

SERVES 4

2   pounds haddock, cut into 8 pieces
    Salt and pepper
3   tablespoons olive oil
2   onions, peeled and finely chopped
4   fresh jalapeño peppers, seeded and minced
      (wear rubber gloves)
4   garlic cloves, peeled and minced
½   cup dry white wine
1   teaspoon coriander seeds, crushed
2   tablespoons peeled minced fresh gingerroot
1   cup dry-roasted unsalted peanuts, ground fine
    Cooked rice

1. Season the fish pieces with salt and pepper to taste.

2. In a large skillet, heat the olive oil and in it sauté the onions and jalapeños over medium-high heat, stirring, for 3 minutes.

3. Push the mixture to one side of the skillet, add the garlic and the fish pieces, and brown the fish for 2 minutes on each side.

4. Add the wine, coriander seeds, gingerroot, and peanuts and simmer the mixture for 2 minutes, or until the fish just flakes.

5. Serve hot on a bed of hot rice.

Mahimahi in Coconut Milk

THIS IS *another recipe I picked up in my travels through the Far East. A British friend who lives in Hong Kong, high on Victoria Peak overlooking the bay, cooked this at his home one beautiful night. Talk about a romantic evening . . . you will note that the recipe for coconut milk is different from an earlier version. That's o.k. There are probably dozens more I've yet to discover.*

SERVES 4

2½ cups coconut milk (see Note)
4 cloves garlic, peeled and minced
1 teaspoon grated fresh gingerroot
4 pecans, ground
2 onions, peeled and chopped
1 small jalapeño pepper, seeded and crushed (wear rubber gloves)
½ teaspoon turmeric
Juice of 1 lemon
2 pounds mahimahi fillets, cut in 1-inch slices
½ lemon, cut in wedges
Cooked rice

1. In a large saucepan, combine the coconut milk, garlic, ginger, pecan meal, onions, jalapeño pepper, turmeric, and lemon juice. Heat over medium-high heat, stirring frequently, until the mixture boils, then lower heat and simmer until the mixture is reduced to 2 cups.

2. Add mahimahi and lemon wedges and continue to simmer, stirring, for about 10 minutes, until the fish barely flakes.

3. Spoon hot rice onto 4 dinner plates, and spoon 4 equal portions of the mahimahi mixture into the center of the rice. Serve hot.

Coconut Milk

MAKES
ABOUT
1½ CUPS

2½   cups milk
2½   cups grated coconut.

1. In a saucepan, combine the milk and grated coconut.

2. Bring to a boil, lower the heat and cook for 2 minutes, then strain and discard the solids

Curried Scallops

YOU MIGHT add raisins or shredded coconut to the accompaniments for this dish. And you might want to serve it with some soft, warm pita bread.

SERVES 4

1   cup dry white wine
1   pound sea scallops, cut in halves
2   tablespoons butter or margarine
2   tablespoons all-purpose flour
2½   teaspoons curry powder
¼   cup Major Grey's chutney

ACCOMPANIMENTS:
Cooked white rice
Chopped scallions
Chopped peanuts

1. In a saucepan, bring the wine to a boil, reduce the heat until the wine is just simmering. Add the scallops, cover the pan, and poach the scallops for 2 or 3 minutes, until they're just firm to the touch. Transfer the scallops with a slotted spoon to a bowl, reserving the cooking liquid.

2. In a small saucepan, melt the butter, add the flour, and cook the roux over low heat for 2 minutes, whisking constantly.

3. Add the curry powder, the chutney, and the reserved cooking liquid and cook the mixture for 1 or 2 minutes, whisking constantly.

4. Stir in the scallops and heat the mixture over low heat, stirring, until the scallops are just heated through, about 1 or 2 minutes.

5. Place a bed of hot, cooked rice on each of 4 plates, spoon the scallop mixture over the rice and sprinkle it with scallions and peanuts. Serve hot.

Seafood Risotto

A WONDERFUL way to brighten up risotto, but the key here is the risotto. As long as that comes out just right, the rest of the recipe is fail-safe. Serve some cold roasted peppers with a vinaigrette dressing as a starter course.

S E R V E S   6

2 tablespoons olive oil
2 onions, peeled and chopped
2 cloves garlic, peeled and minced
½ teaspoon crushed dried red pepper flakes
2 cups Italian Arborio short-grain rice
2 cups dry white wine
2 cups White Fish Stock (page 258)
One 8-ounce can Italian plum tomatoes, drained and crushed
1 tablespoon chopped fresh basil leaves
Salt and pepper
6 clams, thoroughly scrubbed
½ pound crabmeat, picked over
2 lobster tails, cut into 3 sections each
6 medium shrimp, unpeeled
Chopped fresh parsley leaves

1. In a large heavy saucepan, heat the oil over medium-high heat and sauté the onions, garlic, and red pepper flakes until the onions are tender.

2. Add the rice and sauté until the rice is translucent.

3. Add 1 cup wine and cook, stirring, until it is absorbed. Continue to add wine and fish stock alternately in ½-cup portions, stirring occasionally and adding more liquid as necessary until the rice is tender, about 20 minutes.

4. Add the tomatoes and basil and season to taste with salt and pepper.

5. Bring the mixture to a boil, reduce the heat, and add the clams, crabmeat, and lobster meat. Cook about 3 minutes, then add the shrimp and cook 2 minutes more, or until the clams open and the lobster is done. Sprinkle with chopped parsley. Serve hot.

Baked Shrimp Cajun Style

BACK IN *the early 1980s I had the good fortune of appearing each week for almost three years on a television program called "Saturday Morning," which was broadcast every Saturday morning (appropriate, eh?) live in New York. We had a wonderful cast of regulars and each week we also invited a couple of celebrity guests to join us. One week the king of Cajun cookery, Paul Prudhomme, came on the show and prepared this marvelous baked shrimp.*

**S E R V E S 4
T O 6**

1½ pounds shrimp (about 40), shelled and deveined
5 tablespoons butter or margarine
1½ teaspoons chili powder
2 teaspoons freshly ground black pepper
⅛ teaspoon cayenne pepper, or slightly more to taste
2 garlic cloves, peeled and minced
4 teaspoons Worcestershire sauce
¼ cup dry red wine
½ teaspoon salt
Cooked rice

1. Preheat the oven to 425 degrees. Arrange the shrimp in a baking dish.

2. In a saucepan, combine the butter, chili powder, black pepper, cayenne, garlic, Worcestershire sauce, wine, and salt, bring the mixture to a boil, and pour it over the shrimp.

3. Bake the shrimp for 6 to 8 minutes, or until they are just firm.

4. Serve the hot shrimp mixture over cooked rice.

Brazilian Shrimp with Red Peppers

ANOTHER TERRIFIC *shrimp dish worth the little cholesterol binge. Excellent with Spanish rice as well as plain white.*

S E R V E S   4

½ cup olive oil
4 garlic cloves, peeled and thinly sliced
2 large red bell peppers, seeded, ribs removed, and cut into julienne strips
1 hot red pepper, seeded, deveined, and cut into julienne strips (wear rubber gloves.)
3 dozen medium-large shrimp, in their shells
   Hot cooked rice
2 tablespoons chopped fresh cilantro leaves

1. Put half the oil in a skillet and place over moderate heat. Add the garlic and sauté until golden.

2. Add the red peppers and the hot pepper to the skillet and cook until they wilt, about 4 minutes. Remove the peppers with a slotted spoon and set aside.

3. Add the remaining ¼ cup oil to the skillet and raise the heat. When the oil just begins to smoke, add the shrimp and cook until they start to char, about 4 minutes.

4. Place a bed of hot cooked rice on each of 4 plates, arrange the shrimp on the rice, and sprinkle each portion with the garlic, peppers, and cilantro. Serve at once.

Shrimp Creole

NOTHING UNIQUE
about this recipe, but it's
a wonderful old standby
and you should have it in
your repertoire.

S E R V E S   6

2   pounds bay shrimp, cooked, shelled, and
     deveined
3   tablespoons butter or margarine
1   cup chopped onion
1   cup chopped green pepper
1   cup chopped zucchini
2   cloves garlic, peeled and minced
4   large tomatoes, peeled, seeded, and chopped
One 8-ounce can tomato sauce
½   teaspoon black pepper
2   teaspoons grated fresh lemon zest
3   whole cloves
1   bay leaf
½   teaspoon dried thyme
½   teaspoon honey
     Cooked rice
3   tablespoons minced fresh parsley leaves

1. Rinse shrimp in cold water, pat dry, and set aside.

2. In a large saucepan, melt the butter over medium heat, add the onion, green pepper, and zucchini and sauté until the vegetables are tender but not brown.

3. Add garlic and tomatoes and bring the mixture to a boil, stirring occasionally.

4. Reduce the heat and add the tomato sauce, pepper, lemon rind, cloves, bay leaf, thyme, and honey. Simmer for 15 minutes, stirring frequently.

5. Stir in shrimp, heat thoroughly, remove the bay leaf, and serve at once over hot rice. Garnish with parsley.

Halibut Steaks with Tomatoes and Cucumbers

ALTHOUGH MOST *flaky white fish will freeze well, halibut seems to freeze better than most. Whether you use halibut steaks or halibut fillets for this recipe makes no difference—it's a savory experience.*

SERVES 4

½ teaspoon freshly grated lemon zest
3 tablespoons fresh lemon juice
1 teaspoon dried oregano, crumbled
½ cup olive oil
1½ cups cherry tomatoes, halved, seeded, and thinly sliced
1 cup seeded and thinly sliced cucumber
Four 1-inch-thick halibut steaks, about 6 to 8 ounces each

1. Preheat the broiler.

2. In a bowl, whisk together the lemon zest, lemon juice, and oregano, and whisk in the olive oil until the mixture is emulsified. Stir in the tomatoes and the cucumber.

3. Broil the halibut steaks about 5 minutes on each side, or until they are slightly browned and just flake.

4. Transfer the halibut steaks to warm plates and spoon the tomato mixture over them. Serve hot.

Entrées

Broiled Halibut with Sour Cream, Onions, and Mushrooms

THIS RECIPE *could be subtitled Halibut Stroganoff. I like to fool around with sauces that would normally go on meats, or chicken, or pasta, and put them on fish. I've tried this sauce on several different types of fish, but halibut's texture seems best suited to it.*

S E R V E S 4

4　halibut steaks, 6 to 8 ounces each
　Juice of 2 limes
　Salt and pepper
3　tablespoons butter or margarine
1½　cups sliced fresh mushrooms
2　small onions, peeled and sliced
1　cup sour cream or sour cream substitute

1. Place halibut steaks in a shallow glass, ceramic, or enamel dish, squeeze on lime juice, season with salt and pepper to taste, cover, and place in refrigerator to marinate for 1 hour.

2. Preheat the broiler.

3. In a saucepan, melt 2 tablespoons of the butter over medium-high heat and sauté the mushrooms and onions, stirring occasionally, until the mushrooms are just soft and the onions are translucent, about 6 minutes. Lower the heat and keep warm.

4. Place halibut steaks in a greased broiling pan, dot the steaks with the remaining 1 tablespoon of butter, and broil them 6 to 8 inches from the heat for about 10 minutes, turning once, or until they just flake. Remove from oven and place a steak on each of 4 warm dinner plates.

5. Add the sour cream to the mushroom mixture, heat through, stirring, for 2 minutes over medium-high heat, then pour the sauce over the steaks. Serve hot.

Broiled Pesto Halibut with Another Tomato Sauce

PESTO, GENERALLY *a sauce for pasta, is excellent with halibut, swordfish, tuna, or shark. Serve this with corn fritters.*

S E R V E S   4

4   halibut fillets, 6 to 8 ounces each
2   tablespoons olive oil
    Salt and pepper
1   recipe Pesto Sauce (page 251)
1   recipe Another Tomato Sauce (page 252)
    Fresh basil sprigs

1. Preheat the broiler.

2. Rub the halibut fillets with the olive oil, season with salt and pepper to taste, and place in a broiler pan.

3. Coat one side of each fillet generously with pesto sauce, then place the halibut under the preheated broiler, about 6 inches from the heat, and broil without turning for 4 or 5 minutes, until the fish just flakes.

4. Heat the tomato sauce and spoon equal portions among 4 heated dinner plates. Place a halibut fillet in the center of each, pesto side up, and garnish with basil sprigs. Serve hot.

Orange Roughy with Red Pepper Sauce

THERE ARE *several variations on red, green, or yellow bell pepper sauce, and this is one of the most interesting. It's a little tangier than the other sweet pepper sauces in this book, although they are delicious, too.*

S E R V E S   4

2 pounds orange roughy fillets
2 tablespoons olive oil
1 tablespoon chopped shallots
3 cloves garlic, peeled and chopped
6 anchovies
1 tablespoon chopped fresh parsley leaves
2 roasted red peppers, peeled, seeded, and sliced into narrow strips (see Note)
⅛ teaspoon cayenne pepper
2 tablespoons olive oil
Salt and pepper

1. Rinse the orange roughy in cold water, pat dry, cut into 4 equal portions, and set aside. Preheat the broiler.

2. In a small saucepan, heat 2 tablespoons of olive oil, then add the shallots and garlic and sauté until tender but not brown.

3. Add the anchovies and stir to dissolve.

4. Add parsley, red peppers, and cayenne and heat through. Remove the sauce from the heat and keep warm.

5. Baste the orange roughy fillets with olive oil, season with salt and pepper to taste, and place them on a broiling pan.

6. Broil the orange roughy 6 inches from the heat for 5 minutes on each side.

7. With a slotted spatula transfer the fish to 4 plates and top each with some of the red pepper sauce. Serve hot.

NOTE: To roast peppers, preheat your oven to 400 degrees, place the peppers in a baking pan, and roast until the skin begins to char. Remove from oven, wait for the peppers to cool so you can handle them, and remove the skins.

Broiled Mackerel with Rhubarb and Tomato Sauce

RHUBARB HAS *always fascinated me. I once made a foot-long pie because I couldn't find any shorter rhubarb. (Only kidding.) The tangy-sweet taste of this rhubarb-tomato sauce is a perfect foil for the somewhat oily, slightly fishy flavor of the mackerel.*

SERVES 4

2 tablespoons butter or margarine

3 tablespoons chopped onion

1 pound rhubarb, trimmed and cut into ¾-inch slices

1 large tomato, peeled, seeded, and cut into ¼-inch cubes

1 tablespoon sugar

Salt and pepper

2 tablespoons olive or vegetable oil

4 mackerel fillets, 6 to 8 ounces each

¼ teaspoon dried thyme

1. In a saucepan, melt the butter over medium heat and add the onion; sauté for about 2 minutes, until the onion is translucent.

2. Add the rhubarb, tomato, sugar, and salt and pepper to taste, lower the heat, and cook, covered, stirring occasionally, for 6 minutes.

3. Preheat the broiler.

4. Put 1 tablespoon oil in a broiling pan, lay the mackerel fillets in the pan, drizzle them with the remaining 1 tablespoon oil, and sprinkle on the thyme.

5. Broil the mackerel fillets for about 5 or 6 minutes, until they are slightly browned on top and just flake.

6. Transfer the broiled mackerel fillets to a serving platter and serve hot, with the rhubarb and tomato sauce alongside.

Broiled Pollock with Curry and Green Chile Sauce

THIS TASTY *sauce also goes well with cod, sea bass, or halibut.*

S E R V E S   4

1 tablespoon olive oil
2 tablespoon butter or margarine
1 onion, peeled and thinly sliced
1 tablespoon curry powder
½ teaspoon ground ginger
1 cup White Fish Stock (page 258)
1½ teaspoons chopped canned hot green chile pepper
Salt and pepper
¼ cup dry white wine
4 pollock fillets, 6 to 8 ounces each

1. In a large skillet, heat the olive oil and butter over medium-high heat and sauté the onion until it starts to brown.

2. Lower the heat, add the curry powder and ginger, and cook for 3 minutes, stirring occasionally.

3. Add the fish stock and chopped green chile pepper and cook for another 3 minutes, stirring occasionally. Season with salt and pepper to taste, then turn off the heat and set aside, covered, to keep warm.

4. Preheat the broiler.

5. Pour the wine into a broiling pan and lay the pollock fillets in the wine. Broil the fillets for 5 to 7 minutes, until the fish just flakes.

6. Transfer the pollock fillets to a serving platter and spoon the sauce over them. Serve hot.

Broiled Pollock with Shrimp-Butter Sauce

COD, RED snapper, or haddock can be substituted for the pollock in this recipe.

SERVES 4

2 tablespoon butter or margarine
2 tablespoons chopped shallots
¼ pound cooked pink (bay) shrimp, chopped
1 tablespoon fresh thyme or 1 teaspoon dried
Salt and pepper
4 pollock fillets, 6 to 8 ounces each
¼ cup dry white wine
1 teaspoon cornstarch
2 teaspoons chopped fresh parsley leaves

1. Preheat the broiler.

2. In a small skillet, melt the butter over medium heat, add the shallots, the shrimp, and the thyme, season to taste with salt and pepper, and cook for 30 seconds, stirring constantly.

3. Place the pollock fillets in a baking dish and pour the shrimp-butter mixture over them. Broil the pollock fillets for 4 to 6 minutes, or until they just flake.

4. Remove from oven and transfer the pollock fillets to a serving dish. Cover to keep the fish warm. Pour the liquid from the baking dish into a small saucepan.

5. Combine wine and cornstarch and stir into the liquid, cooking and stirring until the mixture thickens.

6. Spoon the sauce over the pollock fillets and garnish with parsley. Serve hot.

Salmon Steaks with Mustard-mint Sauce

THIS IS *a very quick and easy recipe—just make sure to keep tasting the dressing until the balance of mint and mustard is just exactly right.*

S E R V E S   4

⅔ cup mayonnaise
2 tablespoons fresh lemon juice
4 teaspoons coarse-grained Dijon-style mustard
¼ cup shredded fresh mint leaves, or 2 teaspoons dried
4 salmon steaks, 6 to 8 ounces each
   Salt and pepper

1. Whisk the mayonnaise, lemon juice, mustard, mint and 2 tablespoons of water together in a bowl and let stand at room temperature for 15 minutes. Preheat the broiler.

2. Season the salmon steaks with salt and pepper to taste, then broil for about 5 or 6 minutes on each side.

3. Place a broiled salmon steak on each of 4 warm plates and top with mustard-mint sauce. Serve hot.

Broiled Salmon with Tomato Sauce and Garlic Cream

THIS IS *probably the fanciest, most "difficult" recipe in my repertoire. It originated in the kitchen of famed Southwestern chef Robert Del Grande and I only trot it out for the most special occasions. But the oohs and ahhs you'll get from your guests will make it all worthwhile.*

SERVES 4

THE ROASTED TOMATO SAUCE

8   ripe plum tomatoes
1   shallot, peeled
2   cloves garlic, peeled
1   jalapeño pepper, stem removed
¼   cup White Fish Stock (page 258) or water
1   cup loosely packed fresh cilantro leaves
2   tablespoons butter or margarine
    Salt

THE GARLIC CREAM

8   large cloves garlic, unpeeled
2   tablespoons olive oil
⅓   cup sour cream
½   cup cream
½   teaspoon fresh lime juice
    Salt and pepper

4   salmon fillets, 6 to 8 ounces each
    Juice of 1 lime
    Cilantro leaves

1. Preheat the oven to 400 degrees.

2. To make the roasted tomato sauce, place the tomatoes, shallot, garlic cloves, and jalapeño pepper in a small roasting pan and roast them in the preheated oven until the tomatoes are blistered and the shallot is soft, about 30 to 35 minutes. Leave the oven on.

3. Transfer the roasted vegetables to a blender or food processor fitted with the steel blade and purée.

4. Scrape the tomato purée into a saucepan, whisk in the fish stock or water, and bring the mixture to a boil.

5. Reduce the heat to low, chop the cilantro, and add it to the sauce.

6. Add the butter, season with salt to taste, and keep warm over very low heat.

7. To make the garlic cream, place the garlic cloves and olive oil in a small roasting pan. Cover with foil and roast until the garlic is very soft, about 15 or 20 minutes.

8. Remove the garlic cloves from the oven, crush the cloves in a mortar or small bowl, slipping them from out of their skins, then combine the crushed garlic, the olive oil in which it was cooked, the sour cream, cream, and lime juice and mix until smooth. Thin with 1 or 2 table-spoons of water if necessary. Season to taste with salt and pepper. Preheat the broiler.

9. Place the salmon on a broiling pan, sprinkle with the lime juice, and broil the fillets for 3 to 4 minutes on each side, until they just flake.

10. To serve, divide the roasted tomato sauce among 4 dinner plates. Top each portion with a salmon fillet, then drizzle the garlic cream over the salmon and garnish with cilantro leaves. Serve hot.

Grilled Salmon with Leeks and Tarragon-Honey Glaze

SEVERAL OF *my friends have tried this glaze on chicken and say it's just as good on that as it is on the salmon. I'll take their word for it. This is superb with grilled eggplant slices brushed with a teriyaki marinade.*

SERVES 4

6 large leeks
4 tablespoons (½ stick) butter or margarine
  Salt and pepper
½ cup cream or half-and-half
4 salmon fillets, 6 to 8 ounces each
6 tablespoons honey
2 tablespoons grated orange zest
2 tablespoons grated lemon zest
  Juice of 2 lemons
¼ cup fresh tarragon, or 1 tablespoon dried

1. Rinse leeks thoroughly under running cold water. Cut into 1-inch sections.

2. In a skillet, melt the butter over medium-high heat and add the leeks. Sauté for 5 minutes, then add salt and pepper to taste.

3. Add the cream and continue cooking for another 5 minutes, or until the leeks are just tender. Transfer leeks to the center of 4 plates and set aside.

4. Preheat the broiler.

5. Season salmon with salt and pepper.

6. In a blender or food processor fitted with the steel blade, combine the honey, orange and lemon zests, lemon juice, and tarragon and process until smooth. Brush this tarragon-honey glaze onto the salmon fillets, reserving some for basting.

7. Grill or broil the salmon for about 3 minutes on

each side, basting with additional glaze during the cooking.

8. Remove salmon fillets with a slotted spatula and place one on each plate over the leeks. Serve hot.

Broiled Shad Roe

4   shad roes
Salt and pepper
¼ cup melted butter
Lemon wedges

"WAITER, BRING me shad roe . . ." Lyrics from a Cole Porter song. I've tried shad roe on a couple of occasions, once poached and once broiled. I preferred it broiled, and it's worth trying at least once, if you haven't already, just to see what you may have been missing. And nothing, absolutely nothing, could be easier.

SERVES 4

1. Preheat the broiler.

2. Season the roes to taste with salt and pepper. Place them in a greased broiling pan and brush them with the melted butter.

3. Broil the roes 6 inches from the heat source until they are light brown, about 4 to 5 minutes, brushing several times with the butter. Turn the roes over and broil another 4 to 5 minutes, basting with the butter, until golden brown.

4. Transfer the roes to 4 warm dinner plates and serve hot with the lemon wedges.

Shark with Sake and Lemon Juice

WHEN I *had this dish at an absolutely wonderful (and expensive!) restaurant in Kyoto, Japan, they asked each diner to season his or her own fish with the sake, lemon juice, and salt at the table.*

S E R V E S   4

4   mako or black tip shark steaks, 6 to 8 ounces
    each
    Olive oil
    Freshly chopped chives
½   cup warm sake
½   cup fresh lemon juice
    Salt

1. Preheat the broiler.

2. Rub the shark steaks with olive oil.

3. Place the steaks in a broiling pan, and broil them 6 inches from the heat source for 5 minutes on each side, or until they are browned on top.

4. Place each steak on a dinner plate and serve hot, inviting each diner to spoon sake, lemon juice, and salt over the steaks to taste.

Shark Steaks with Parsley-Walnut Sauce

A DEAR *friend once told me that even though it was a bit of a chore, any time a recipe called for walnuts you should peel them, because walnut skin is slightly bitter. I leave it up to you, but my friend was right: If you want this "parsley pesto sauce" to be perfect, you've got to peel the walnuts. This dish is excellent served with baked sweet potato chunks.*

SERVES 4

4   shark steaks, 6 to 8 ounces each
2   cups milk
1   cup loosely packed fresh parsley leaves
2   garlic cloves, peeled and minced
2   tablespoons chopped walnuts, lightly toasted
½   cup grated Parmesan cheese
½   cup plus 2 tablespoons olive oil
    Salt and pepper
    Fresh lime juice
    Parsley sprigs

1. Place the shark steaks in a large broiling pan in one layer, add the milk, cover with aluminum foil or plastic wrap, and allow to soak for 1 hour in the refrigerator.

2. While the shark is soaking, in a blender or food processor fitted with the steel blade purée the parsley, garlic cloves, walnuts, Parmesan cheese, and ½ cup of the olive oil. Set aside.

3. Preheat the broiler.

4. Drain the shark steaks and pat them dry. Brush them with the remaining 2 tablespoons of olive oil, season with salt and pepper to taste, then broil them for about 5 minutes on each side, or until tender when tested with a fork.

5. Spoon equal amounts of the parsley-walnut sauce onto 4 warm plates, then place a shark steak on top of each puddle of sauce. Drizzle fresh lime juice over each steak and garnish with parsley sprigs. Serve hot.

Broiled Shark Steaks with Green Olive Tapenade

UNTIL I *made this dish I really wasn't mentally ready to substitute shark for swordfish. Now I serve shark all the time, and I've converted a lot of my doubting friends.*

S E R V E S 4

T H E T A P E N A D E

1   cup pimiento-stuffed green olives, chopped fine
1   tablespoon drained capers
4   anchovy fillets, minced
1   teaspoon fresh lemon juice
1   garlic clove, peeled and minced
¼   teaspoon dried thyme, crumbled
    Freshly ground pepper

Four   1-inch-thick shark steaks, about 6 to 8 ounces each
2   tablespoons olive oil
    Freshly ground pepper
2   tablespoons fine breadcrumbs

1. Preheat the broiler.

2. To make the tapenade, in a bowl combine the olives, capers, anchovies, lemon juice, garlic, thyme, and freshly ground pepper to taste. Set aside.

3. Rub the shark steaks with 1 tablespoon of the olive oil, season each with pepper, and broil them in a broiling pan, turning them once, for 10 minutes, or until they are tender when tested with a fork.

4. Spread the tapenade on top of the shark steaks, sprinkle them with the breadcrumbs, and drizzle the topping with the remaining 1 tablespoon of oil.

5. Broil the shark steaks for 2 more minutes, or until the crumbs are golden brown. Serve hot.

Swordfish Steaks with Red and Yellow Pepper Sauces

THE FIRST *time I saw this combination, red bell pepper sauce on the left side of the plate, yellow bell pepper sauce on the right, the two joining in a perfect line in the center and a piece of broiled swordfish nestled on top, was in a hotel in Detroit. The next time was at my dining table.*

SERVES 4

THE PEPPER SAUCES

2 large red bell peppers
2 large yellow bell peppers
4 shallots, peeled and chopped
¼ cup dry white wine
1 cup White Fish Stock (page 258)
2 teaspoons dry sherry
Salt
Pinch cayenne pepper

4 swordfish steaks, 6 to 8 ounces each
Olive oil
Salt and freshly ground black pepper
Parsley sprigs

1. To make the pepper sauces, put the red and yellow peppers in a baking pan in a preheated 425-degree oven. Roast for 15 minutes, turning occasionally, or until the pepper skin is charred and easy to peel.

2. Remove the peppers from the oven and, when they are cool enough to handle, slip off the skins, discard the ribs and seeds, and cut into chunks or strips, keeping the red and yellow peppers separate.

3. Put the red pepper chunks, half the shallots, half the wine, and half the stock in a blender or food processor fitted with the steel blade. Purée.

4. Transfer the puréed red pepper mixture to a

saucepan and, over medium-high heat, reduce to the consistency of thick cream. Add half the sherry and season with salt and cayenne.

5. Repeat with the chunks of yellow pepper.

6. Preheat the broiler.

7. Rub the swordfish steaks with olive oil, season with salt and pepper to taste, then arrange them in a broiling pan. Broil the fish about 6 inches from the heat source for 4 to 5 minutes on each side, or until the fish just barely flakes.

8. Spoon red and yellow pepper sauces onto 4 warm dinner plates so each covers half the plate. Place a swordfish steak in the center of each plate, and garnish with parsley sprigs. Serve hot.

Grilled Swordfish with Papaya Sauce

SOMETIMES A *recipe can look intimidating simply because of its length. This is one of those, but believe me, it's worth the effort if you have the time. The results are breathtaking to look at and sensational to eat—a true upscale restaurant-type dish that will impress even your most blasé dinner guests.*

SERVES 4

2 cups lightly packed fresh basil leaves
2 cups lightly packed fresh parsley leaves
1 tablespoon fresh rosemary, or 1 teaspoon dried
1 tablespoon fresh thyme, or 1 teaspoon dried
1 onion, peeled and quartered
4 garlic cloves, peeled and halved
1 cup olive oil
½ teaspoon salt
Four 1-inch thick swordfish steaks, 6 to 8 ounces each
1 beet, peeled, cut into julienne strips, and reserved in a bowl of ice water
1 papaya, halved, seeded, and the pulp scooped out
1 tablespoon fresh lemon juice
2 cups dry white wine
1 bay leaf
1 shallot, peeled and minced
½ cup cream or half-and-half
½ pound (2 sticks) butter or margarine, cut into pieces and softened
½ teaspoon Worcestershire sauce
White pepper
Vegetable oil for brushing grill pan

1. In a blender or food processor fitted with the steel blade purée the basil with the parsley, rosemary, thyme, onion, garlic, and the olive oil. Add ¼ teaspoon of the salt and transfer the marinade to a dish or pan large enough to hold the swordfish in one layer.

2. Add the swordfish, turn it to coat it well, and chill, covered, for at least 6 hours. Let the swordfish stand in the marinade at room temperature for 30 minutes before cooking it.

3. Peel and julienne the beet and set aside.

4. In a blender or food processor fitted with the steel blade purée the papaya. Transfer the purée to a small bowl and stir in 2 teaspoons of the lemon juice.

5. In a small saucepan, bring the wine to a boil with the bay leaf and the shallot, and boil the mixture until the wine is reduced to about ½ cup.

6. Add the cream, boil the mixture until it is reduced to about ½ cup, and discard the bay leaf.

7. Reduce the heat to low and whisk in the butter, 1 piece at a time.

8. Stir in the remaining 1 teaspoon lemon juice, the Worcestershire sauce, the remaining ¼ teaspoon salt, and the white pepper to taste, strain the mixture through a fine sieve into a clean saucepan, and discard the solids.

9. Whisk in 2 tablespoons of the papaya purée and keep the sauce warm, covered. Reserve remaining papaya purée.

10. Brush a large ridged grill pan or cast-iron skillet lightly with the vegetable oil and in it grill the swordfish, drained (but don't wipe off the marinade coating), over high heat for 5 minutes. Turn the swordfish with a spatula and grill for 5 minutes more, or until it is just cooked through.

11. Divide the papaya sauce among 4 heated plates and arrange the swordfish on it.

12. Spoon the remaining papaya purée around the swordfish, swirl the purée into the sauce with a toothpick, and arrange the julienned beet decoratively around each serving. Serve hot.

Tuna with Tomato, Green Pepper and Basil Sauce

JUST A *reminder: No matter how careful you are about preparing this, or any tuna recipe, it will all be for naught if the tuna is overcooked. In order to be edible (for me, anyway), tuna must be rare—warm sashimi at the center, if you will.*

S E R V E S   4

¼ cup olive oil

1 cup chopped onion

3 cloves garlic, peeled and chopped

1 green pepper, seeded and ribs removed, finely chopped

4 medium tomatoes, peeled, seeded, and cut into ½-inch cubes

   Salt and pepper

½ cup dry white wine

4 tuna steaks, about 8 ounces each

3 tablespoons butter or margarine, melted

½ cup fresh basil leaves, cut into julienne strips

1. In a saucepan, heat the oil over medium heat. Add the onion and garlic and sauté, stirring occasionally, until the onion is translucent.

2. Add the green pepper and sauté for 3 minutes.

3. Add the tomatoes and salt and pepper to taste. Cover the pan, lower the heat, and simmer the sauce for 10 minutes.

4. Preheat the broiler.

5. Pour the white wine into a broiling pan and lay the tuna steaks in the pan.

6. Spoon the melted butter over the tuna and broil the steaks until they are just barely cooked through, about 5 to 6 minutes, turning once.

7. Remove the tuna steaks from the oven and transfer them with a slotted spatula to 4 heated plates.

8. Stir the basil strips into the sauce and serve the sauce on the side. Serve hot.

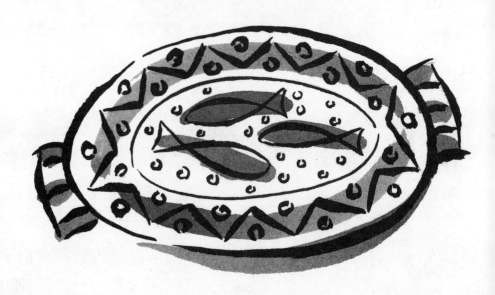

Grilled Ocean Whitefish with Marinated Peppers and Tomatillos

A TOMATILLO is pretty much what it sounds like— a small Spanish tomato. A green tomato, that is, with a very thin husk. They are available at Latin markets, specialty food stores, and better markets. This recipe—as is true for almost any grilled dish—can be done on an outdoor barbecue or indoor grill.

SERVES 4

THE MARINADE

2 red bell peppers, seeded, ribs removed, and cut into 1-inch-long julienne strips

2 yellow bell peppers, seeded, ribs removed, and cut into 1-inch-long julienne strips

2 green bell peppers, seeded, ribs removed, and cut into 1-inch-long julienne strips

4 tomatillos, husked and cut into 1/8-inch-thick wedges

3 jalapeño peppers, seeded and minced (wear rubber gloves)

1/2 cup olive oil

1/2 cup fresh lime juice

2 bunches fresh cilantro, stemmed and minced

4 ocean whitefish fillets, 6 to 8 ounces each

1/4 cup olive oil

Salt and pepper

1. To make the marinade, toss the bell pepper strips, tomatillos, and jalapeño peppers with 1/2 cup olive oil and the lime juice in a large nonreactive bowl. Let stand for 2 hours.

2. Add the cilantro to the bell pepper mixture and prepare the grill.

3. Brush both sides of the whitefish with 1/4 cup oil and season with salt and pepper to taste.

4. Transfer fish to the grill rack and cook for 2 or 3 minutes per side, or until it just begins to flake.

5. Arrange fillets on warm plates and spoon the pepper marinade over them. Serve hot.

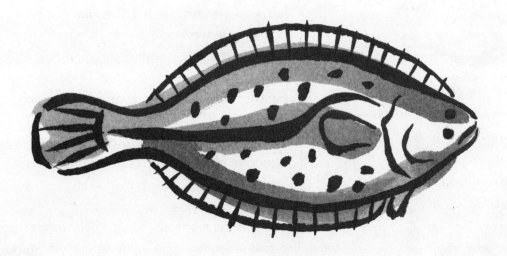

Poached, Simmered, or Stewed

Flounder in Tomato-Mushroom Sauce

THIS RECIPE *works equally well with halibut, whitefish, cod, and pollock. Serve with steamed Chinese snow peas.*

S E R V E S   4

1 tablespoon butter or margarine

2 leeks, white and pale green part only, well
  rinsed, trimmed, and thinly sliced

2 shallots, peeled and finely chopped

2 scallions, green tops removed, thinly sliced

1 pound fresh mushrooms, cleaned and chopped

2 tomatoes, seeded and chopped

3 tablespoons chopped fresh parsley leaves

2 teaspoons dried thyme, crumbled

1 teaspoon dried marjoram

1½ cups cream or half-and-half

4 flounder fillets, 6 to 8 ounces each
  Salt and pepper

1. Put the butter, leeks, shallots, scallions, mushrooms, tomato, 1 tablespoon of the parsley, thyme, and marjoram in a large skillet. Add ¼ cup water and simmer over medium-low heat for 6 to 8 minutes, stirring occasionally, until the vegetables are softened and the liquid has evaporated.

2. Add the cream to the skillet and simmer gently.

3. Season the flounder fillets with salt and pepper to taste and place the fish in the skillet. Spoon the sauce over the fillets and cook over medium-low heat for 6 to 8 minutes, covered until the fish just flakes.

4. Remove the flounder fillets to a heated platter, spoon the sauce over them, and garnish with the remaining 2 tablespoons parsley. Serve hot.

Halibut Steaks in Sauce Piquante

THIS IS *a classic combination, truly a meal in itself, with perhaps a salad and some pumpernickel bread.*

S E R V E S   4

2	tablespoons olive oil
1	onion, peeled and chopped
1	green bell pepper, seeded, ribs removed, and chopped
1	rib celery, trimmed and chopped
1	large garlic clove, peeled and sliced
2	cups White Fish Stock (page 258)
One	28-ounce can Italian plum tomatoes, with their juice
¼	teaspoon cayenne pepper
4	halibut steaks, about 6 to 8 ounces each
¼	cup thinly sliced scallion greens
	Cooked white rice

1. In a saucepan large enough to hold the halibut steaks in one layer, heat the olive oil and sauté the onion, bell pepper, and celery over medium heat, stirring occasionally, until the vegetables are softened.

2. Stir in the garlic and continue to sauté, stirring, for 1 minute.

3. Stir in the fish stock, the tomatoes with their juice, and the cayenne and cook the mixture, stirring occasionally and breaking up the tomatoes, for 1 hour.

4. Add the halibut steaks and simmer them, covered, turning them once, for 6 minutes.

5. Transfer the halibut steaks with a slotted spatula

Entrées

. . .

to a shallow heated dish and boil the sauce, stirring frequently, until it is thickened.

6. Spoon the sauce around the halibut, sprinkle the fish with the scallion greens, and serve hot with rice.

Mahimahi with Cucumber Cream

COOL AND *subtle, this makes a wonderful summertime dish. Serve with some warm slices of fresh papaya for an absolutely wonderful treat.*

S E R V E S   4

4 large cucumbers, peeled, halved lengthwise, and seeded
1 cup White Fish Stock (page 258)
2 cups cream or half-and-half
4 mahimahi fillets, 6 to 8 ounces each
  Salt and pepper
  Parsley sprigs

1. Cut 6 of the cucumber halves crosswise into ¼-inch-thick slices

2. In a large skillet, bring the fish stock to a boil over medium-high heat, and boil until reduced by ⅓.

3. Add cream and cook, over medium heat, stirring, until the mixture has thickened. Reduce heat to low so that sauce barely simmers.

4. Add the sliced cucumbers and cook them until they are just tender, not mushy—about 6 minutes.

5. Add the mahimahi fillets to the cream sauce and turn to coat with the sauce. Cover and cook for 5 minutes, or until the fish just flakes.

6. Using a slotted spatula, transfer the mahimahi fillets to 4 hot dinner plates and keep warm.

7. Grate the reserved cucumber into the cream sauce. Stir and cook for 2 minutes. Season with salt and pepper to taste and then pour the sauce over the mahimahi fillets, arranging the cucumber pieces around and on top of the fish. Garnish with parsley. Serve hot.

Monkfish with Saffron Sauce

THIS RECIPE *combines the "poor man's lobster" with the "rich man's spice." Saffron, which comes from the center of crocus flowers, is as pricey as any spice can get, but as a once-in-a-blue-moon gourmet treat, it's worth it. Accentuate this dish by serving small bowls of crisp steamed spinach alongside.*

S E R V E S   4

1   tablespoon butter or margarine
4   shallots, peeled and minced
1   pound tomatoes, peeled, seeded, and diced
    Salt and pepper
⅔   cup cream or half-and-half
⅓   cup dry vermouth
¼   teaspoon saffron threads, crumbled
1½ pounds monkfish fillets, cut crosswise into
        ¾-inch pieces
1   tablespoon minced fresh parsley leaves

1. In a large skillet, melt the butter over moderately low heat and sauté the shallots, stirring, until they are softened.

2. Add the tomatoes and salt and pepper to taste, and cook the mixture over medium-high heat, stirring, for 3 to 5 minutes, or until most of the liquid from the tomatoes is evaporated.

3. Stir in the cream, vermouth, and saffron and bring the mixture to a boil.

4. Reduce the heat and add the monkfish. Simmer for 6 to 8 minutes, or until it is cooked through.

5. Transfer the monkfish with a slotted spoon to a platter and keep it warm, covered.

6. Boil the sauce, stirring occasionally, until it is thick enough to coat a spoon.

7. Pour off any liquid from the platter, spoon some of the sauce over the monkfish, and sprinkle with the parsley. Serve the remaining sauce separately. Serve hot.

Mussels à la Marinière

THE MUSSELS *must be thoroughly washed and scraped, making sure the "beard," the silky filament by which the mussels attach themselves to rocks, and any vegetation is removed.*

SERVES 4

1   onion, chopped
4   sprigs parsley
¼   teaspoon dried thyme
2   quarts mussels, scrubbed and debearded
6   tablespoons (¾ stick) butter or margarine
    Freshly ground black pepper
1   cup white wine
    Chopped fresh parsley leaves
    Salt

1. Put the onion, parsley sprigs, and thyme in a large kettle.

2. Add the mussels, 3 tablespoons of the butter, and fresh pepper to taste.

3. Add the wine, cover, and steam over medium heat just until the mussels open. (Any mussels that do not open should be thrown away.) Transfer the mussels to a large bowl.

4. To the broth, add the remaining 3 tablespoons butter and some chopped parsley, season with salt to taste, and pour the broth over the mussels. Serve hot with thick French or sourdough bread to sop up the juice.

Poached Orange Roughy with Tomato-Butter Sauce

A GOOD *sauce should enhance the taste of the fish, not disguise it. Although I love orange roughy simply grilled with a little garlic and lemon juice, this tomato sauce is a perfect complement—and some broccoli steamed al dente makes an ideal side dish.*

S E R V E S   4

1   pound plum tomatoes, peeled, seeded, and chopped (or canned plum tomatoes, drained)
3   tablespoons chopped shallots
2   tablespoons fresh lime juice
8   tablespoons (1 stick) butter or margarine, cut into pieces
1   cup dry white wine
8   lime slices
4   orange roughy fillets, 6 to 8 ounces each
4   teaspoons minced fresh parsley leaves

1. In a blender or food processor fitted with the steel blade, purée the tomatoes, shallots, and lime juice.

2. Transfer the purée to a small saucepan and cook over medium heat, stirring occasionally, for 10 to 12 minutes, or until it is very thick.

3. Reduce the heat to low and whisk in the butter, one piece at a time. Reserve the sauce, covered.

4. In a large skillet, combine the wine and the lime slices and heat to a simmer.

5. Add the orange roughy to the simmering liquid, cover, and poach for 4 or 5 minutes, or until the fish just begins to flake.

6. Transfer the orange roughy fillets to 4 heated plates and spoon an equal amount of the reserved sauce over each fillet. Top each fillet with 2 of the lime slices from the skillet and sprinkle each with parsley. Serve hot.

Poached Oysters with Cilantro Butter, Mushrooms and Bell Peppers

I FIRST tasted this dish in a small inn along the coast of Maine. Every time I make it I can hear the ocean thundering on the rocks. Serve this with a big loaf of warm sourdough bread.

S E R V E S   8

10 tablespoons (1 stick plus 2 tablespoons) butter or margarine
1 pound mushrooms, sliced thin
2 large red bell peppers, seeded and cut crosswise into 1/8-inch rings
  Salt
4 dozen oysters, shucked, reserving the liquor
1/2 cup dry white wine
3 cups fresh cilantro leaves, puréed in a blender or food processor fitted with the steel blade

1. In a large skillet, melt 2 tablespoons of the butter or margarine over medium heat and sauté the mushrooms, stirring, for 3 to 4 minutes, or until their liquid has evaporated. Transfer the mushrooms to a plate with a slotted spoon and keep them warm, covered.

2. In the same skillet, simmer the bell peppers in 3 tablespoons water with salt to taste, stirring, for 1 minute, or until they are just wilted, and keep them warm, covered.

3. In a saucepan, combine 1/2 cup of the reserved oyster liquor with the wine, bring the liquid to a boil, skimming with a slotted spoon, and boil it until it is reduced to about 1/2 cup.

4. Whisk in the remaining butter, cut into pieces, a piece at a time. Keep the butter sauce warm, covered.

5. In a large saucepan, combine the oysters with the

remaining liquor and cook them over high heat, skimming the froth with a slotted spoon, for 2 minutes, or until their edges just start to curl.

6. Divide the mushrooms among 8 dinner plates, arranging them in a circle on each plate.

7. Cut the bell pepper rings in half and arrange them around the inside and outside of the circle of mushrooms.

8. Drain the oysters and divide them among the plates, mounding them in the center.

9. Stir the cilantro purée into the butter sauce and spoon 2 or 3 tablespoons of the sauce over the oysters on each plate. Serve hot.

Poached Red Snapper in Carrot-Sherry Sauce

THIS SAUCE *is just as good served on sole, flounder, whitefish, or scrod.*

SERVES 4

THE SAUCE

2 tablespoons butter

2 carrots, finely grated (about 1 cup)

4 teaspoons flour

¼ cup dry sherry

½ cup cream or half-and-half

¼ cup fresh lemon juice

½ cup dry white wine

1 bay leaf, crumbled

¼ teaspoon dried thyme

4 red snapper fillets, 6 to 8 ounces each
Chopped fresh chives or scallion greens

1. To make the sauce, melt the butter in a saucepan over medium heat, add the carrot, and cook for 3 minutes, stirring frequently.

2. Add flour, whisking until blended.

3. Stir in sherry and simmer 4 minutes, stirring occasionally.

4. Add the cream, whisking constantly, and cook until the sauce has thickened. Keep warm.

5. In a skillet, combine the lemon juice, wine, and ¼ cup water, and bring to a simmer over medium-low heat. Add the bay leaf and thyme.

6. Put the red snapper fillets in the skillet, cover, and simmer gently for 4 to 6 minutes, or until they just flake.

7. Remove fillets from skillet with a slotted spoon, lay each on a heated plate, and spoon on the carrot-sherry sauce. Garnish with chopped chives or scallions. Serve hot.

Poached Red Snapper with Crispy Shrimp Topping

THIS IS *another one of those dishes that makes you feel like a chef in a trendy restaurant. The first time I served this to company, there were exclamations all around—before and after they tasted it.*

S E R V E S   4

T H E   M A R I N A D E

¼ cup fresh lemon juice

½ cup dry white wine

1 garlic clove, peeled and minced

½ cup olive oil

Salt and pepper

4 red snapper fillets, 6 to 8 ounces each

T H E   T O P P I N G

½ pound shrimp (about 12 to 14) cooked, shelled, deveined, and chopped

¼ cup minced onion

2 garlic cloves, peeled and minced

¼ cup minced fresh cilantro leaves

1 tablespoon drained capers, chopped fine

¼ teaspoon dried basil, crumbled

¼ teaspoon dried tarragon, crumbled

1 cup cracker crumbs

¼ cup mayonnaise

⅓ cup freshly grated Parmesan cheese

Lemon wedges

1. In a bowl, whisk together all the marinade ingredients.

2. In a glass or enamel dish large enough to hold all the fillets in one layer, combine the snapper fillets with all but ¼ cup of the marinade, cover, and chill, turning them once for 2 hours.

3. In a bowl, stir together the shrimp, onion, garlic, cilantro, capers, basil, tarragon, cracker crumbs, mayonnaise, Parmesan, and the remaining ¼ cup marinade. Set aside.

4. Remove the red snapper fillets from the refrigerator. Pour the marinade plus ¼ cup water into a large saucepan and in it poach the fillets, covered, for 4 to 6 minutes, or until they just flake. Meanwhile, preheat the broiler.

5. Transfer the red snapper fillets to a baking pan, spread them evenly with the shrimp topping, and broil the fillets for about 3 minutes, or until the topping is golden and crisp.

6. Transfer to 4 heated plates and garnish with lemon wedges. Serve hot.

Poached Salmon with Cumin Sauce

POACHED SALMON *is just about my favorite fish dish—hot or cold. I often make salmon salad from it just by adding some chopped scallions and a bit of mayonnaise. Salmon salad made from leftovers of this recipe is especially wonderful.*

S E R V E S   4

1   tablespoon butter or margarine
¼   cup minced shallot
2   teaspoons ground cumin
1   teaspoon celery seeds
3   fresh or canned plum tomatoes, chopped
⅔   cup dry white wine
4   salmon fillets, 6 to 8 ounces each
⅔   cup cream or half-and-half
    Salt and pepper

1. In a skillet large enough to hold the salmon fillets in one layer, combine the butter, shallot, cumin, celery seeds, tomatoes, wine, and ½ cup water, and heat to boiling.

2. Reduce heat and add the salmon fillets. Poach, covered, for about 6 minutes, until the salmon just flakes. Transfer the salmon with a slotted spatula to a platter and cover with foil to keep warm.

3. Boil the poaching liquid until it's reduced to about ¾ cup.

4. Add the cream and salt and pepper to taste and boil the mixture until it has thickened, stirring constantly.

5. Transfer the salmon fillets to 4 hot plates and strain the sauce over each fillet. Serve hot.

Salmon Poached in Orange Juice and Wine

OF ALL *the methods of cooking fish, the simplest, and in many cases the most effective, is poaching. I suggest you use salmon fillets, not salmon steaks, for this dish. The latter are better broiled or grilled.*

SERVES 4

2 cups orange juice
   Juice of 1 lemon
1 cup dry white wine
1 teaspoon dried dill weed or 10 sprigs fresh dill, chopped
4 salmon fillets, 6 to 8 ounces each
1 tablespoon butter

1. Put orange juice, lemon juice, and wine in a deep skillet and heat to boiling. Allow to boil until about ¼ of the poaching liquid has evaporated.

2. Add dill and salmon fillets and cover. Poach for 5 minutes over gentle heat, or until the salmon just begins to flake.

3. Add butter to the pan, continue to cook for 1 more minute, then remove salmon fillets with a slotted spatula. Serve hot, at room temperature, or cold.

Scrod with Broccoli- Cream Sauce

THIS RECIPE *will work equally well with hake, cod, or even halibut fillets. Serve it with small boiled new potatoes.*

S E R V E S 4

1 ½ cups trimmed and chopped broccoli, plus ¼ cup small broccoli florets
2 tablespoons butter or margarine
1 red bell pepper, seeded, ribs removed and minced
½ cup minced onion
1 cup dry white wine
4 scrod fillets, 6 to 8 ounces each
¼ cup cream or half-and-half
Salt and pepper

1. Cook the chopped broccoli in 4 cups boiling water until it is tender. Drain it, reserving 3 cups of the cooking liquid, and set aside in a bowl.

2. In a saucepan, melt 1 tablespoon of the butter over medium-high heat and sauté the bell pepper, stirring occasionally, for 2 minutes, or until it is softened. Keep the pepper warm, covered.

3. Combine the onion, the wine, and the reserved broccoli liquid in a large skillet, bring the liquid to a boil, and simmer for 10 minutes.

4. Add the scrod fillets and poach them at a bare simmer, covered, turning the fillets once, for 5 or 6 minutes, or until they just flake. With a slotted spatula transfer the scrod to a plate and keep warm, covered.

5. Strain ½ cup of the onion, wine, and broccoli liquid into a blender or food processor fitted with the steel blade and purée it with the cooked broccoli, the cream, and salt and pepper to taste.

6. Transfer the sauce to a saucepan and cook it over low heat, stirring, until it is heated through.

7. In a small saucepan of boiling water, blanch the broccoli florets for 1 minute, drain them, and in a small bowl toss them with the remaining 1 tablespoon butter.

8. Cover the bottom of a heated platter with a portion of the sauce, arrange the scrod fillets on top, and garnish the platter with the broccoli florets and 2 tablespoons of the bell pepper. Add the remaining bell pepper to the remaining sauce and serve it with the scrod. Serve hot.

Scrod in Parsley Sauce with Clams

I FIRST ran across this combination of scrod and clams in a tiny restaurant on the Santa Monica pier. It's a delicious meal when served with a crisp mixed green salad with a tangy walnut oil and balsamic vinegar dressing and some warm olive bread.

SERVES 6

½ cup olive oil
4 garlic cloves, peeled and minced
2 cups chopped fresh parsley leaves
3 tablespoons all-purpose flour
6 scrod fillets, about 6 to 8 ounces each
36 littleneck clams, scrubbed
1½ cups dry white wine
Salt and pepper

1. Scrub the clams thoroughly under cold water, discarding any that have cracked shells or that are not tightly shut.

2. In a large skillet, heat the oil until it's hot but not smoking.

3. Add the garlic, 1 cup of the parsley, and the flour and cook the mixture, stirring constantly, for 2 minutes.

4. Add the scrod in one layer, the clams, and the wine, bring the liquid to a simmer, and simmer the mixture, covered, for 5 minutes, or until the scrod just flakes. Transfer the scrod with a slotted spatula to a plate and keep it warm, covered.

5. Add the remaining 1 cup parsley to the clams and cook, covered, over medium-high heat for 2 minutes, or until the clams open. Discard any unopened clams.

6. Season the sauce with salt and pepper to taste, and divide the scrod, the clams, and the sauce among 6 soup plates. Serve hot.

Scrod Fillets in Spicy Yogurt Sauce

WHEN I *was first getting into fish cookery, and still making lots of vegetarian dishes and sauces, I had some interesting spicy yogurt sauce in the refrigerator that I'd used the night before on a plate of steamed veggies. I tried it on a piece of scrod I sautéed, and it was so good that, as they say in show business, I kept it in the act.*

S E R V E S   4

4   scrod fillets, about 6 to 8 ounces each
    All-purpose flour
    Salt and pepper
¼   cup olive oil
2   onions, peeled and thinly sliced
4   garlic cloves, peeled and minced
¼   teaspoon turmeric
¼   teaspoon ground ginger
⅛   teaspoon cinnamon
⅛   teaspoon ground cloves
¼   teaspoon dried hot red pepper flakes
1   cup plain yogurt
¼   cup minced fresh coriander

1. Dredge the scrod in the flour seasoned with salt and pepper. Shake off the excess.

2. In a large skillet, heat 2 tablespoons of the oil over medium-high heat and in it sauté the scrod, turning it once, for 1 or 2 minutes, or until it is browned.

3. Transfer the scrod with a slotted spatula to a platter.

4. Add the remaining 2 tablespoons of olive oil to the skillet and in it sauté the onions over medium heat, stirring occasionally, until they are golden.

5. Stir in the garlic, turmeric, ginger, cinnamon, cloves, and red pepper flakes and cook the mixture, stirring, for 1 minute.

6. Remove the skillet from the heat, stir in the yogurt, and purée the mixture in a blender or food processor fitted with the steel blade until it is smooth.

7. Return the mixture to the skillet, add the scrod, and cook, covered, at a bare simmer, turning the scrod once, for 6 minutes, or until the scrod just flakes.

8. Transfer the fish and sauce to a platter and sprinkle with the coriander. Serve hot.

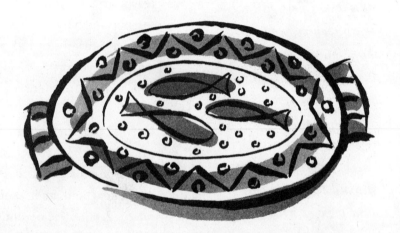

Skate with Black Butter

QUITE FRANKLY, I don't eat a lot of skate, simply because I don't come upon it very often out here on the West Coast. But I buy it when I see it, and this very simple recipe brings out all the rich, subtle flavor of this fish. Baked butternut squash makes a nice accompanying dish.

S E R V E S 4

T H E   B L A C K   B U T T E R

6 tablespoons (¾ stick) butter or margarine
2 tablespoons white wine vinegar
3 tablespoons capers, drained

4 pieces trimmed skate wings, about 6 to 8 ounces each
½ teaspoon salt
¼ cup white wine vinegar
1 onion, peeled and halved
1 bay leaf
6 peppercorns

1. To make the black butter, heat the butter in a saucepan over medium-high heat until it is deep brown but not burned.

2. Add the vinegar and capers, and stir to blend. Keep warm.

3. Rinse the skate wings.

4. In a large saucepan, combine 1 quart water, salt, vinegar, onion, bay leaf, and peppercorns. Bring to a simmer and cook for 10 minutes.

5. Add the skate wings, turn heat to low, and cook for 8 to 10 minutes, or until the fish is white and firm to the touch.

6. Transfer the skate wings to 4 warm plates and spoon the black butter over them. Serve hot.

Sea Bass with Caper-cream Sauce

AT FIRST glance the elements of this recipe seemed strange to me—champagne, Worcestershire sauce, mustard, and capers? But it's delicious, and very quick and easy.

SERVES 4

2 tablespoons butter or margarine
4 sea bass fillets, 6 to 8 ounces each
1 cup heavy cream or half-and-half
2 tablespoons champagne or dry white wine
1 tablespoon Worcestershire sauce
1 tablespoon Dijon-style mustard
2 tablespoons drained capers
   Salt and pepper

1. In a large skillet, heat the butter over moderately high heat and sauté the bass, turning it once, for 1 minute. Transfer it with a slotted spatula to a plate.

2. Into the butter remaining in the skillet stir the cream, champagne, Worcestershire sauce, mustard, capers, and salt and pepper to taste.

3. Return the bass fillets to the skillet and simmer the mixture for 5 to 6 minutes, or until the bass just flakes.

4. Transfer the bass fillets to 4 plates and top each with 2 or 3 tablespoons of the sauce. Serve hot.

Sea Bass with Puréed Vegetables and Caviar

ONE OF *my cousin Neil's creations, bless his heart. And to think he only got interested in fish cookery about the time I started to write this book!*

S E R V E S   6

4   tablespoons (½ stick) butter or margarine
1   cup minced onion
1   cup minced celery
1   cup minced carrot
¼   cup chopped fresh parsley leaves
3   bay leaves
2   whole cloves
    Salt and pepper
½   cup dry white wine
6   sea bass fillets, 6 to 8 ounces each
1   cup White Fish Stock (page 258)
½   cup cream or half-and-half
2   teaspoons fresh lime juice
2   teaspoons fresh lemon juice
¼   cup black caviar
1   hard-boiled egg, chopped
2   tablespoons minced chives

1. In a large skillet, melt the butter over medium-high heat and sauté the onion, celery, and carrot until the vegetables are soft.

2. Add the parsley, bay leaves, cloves, and salt and pepper to taste and cook, covered, over low heat for 15 minutes.

3. Add the white wine and simmer, uncovered, for 5 minutes.

4. Remove the bay leaves and purée the mixture in a blender or food processor fitted with the steel blade.

5. In a skillet, poach the sea bass in the fish stock until tender. Transfer the sea bass fillets with a slotted spatula to a platter and keep warm, covered.

6. To the fish stock, add the puréed vegetables cream, lime juice, and lemon juice, then simmer, stirring constantly, for 2 minutes.

7. Remove from heat and add 2 tablespoons caviar.

8. Pour the sauce over the fish, and top each fillet with 1 teaspoon caviar. Sprinkle with chopped egg and minced chives. Serve hot.

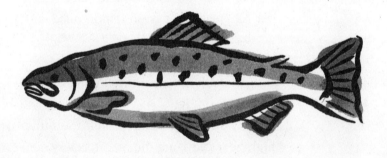

Sea Bass Provençale

THIS ALSO works very well with halibut fillets.

S E R V E S 4

2 tablespoons olive oil
¾ cup chopped onion
2 cloves garlic, minced
One 28-ounce can Italian plum tomatoes, drained and chopped
4 anchovy fillets, drained and finely chopped
½ cup dry white wine
¼ teaspoon dried hot red pepper flakes
1 teaspoon dried thyme, crumbled
4 sea bass fillets, 6 to 8 ounces each
⅔ cup black olives, pitted and sliced
1 tablespoon capers, drained
Salt and pepper
1 tablespoon shredded fresh basil leaves

1. In a large skillet, heat the oil over moderately low heat and sauté the onion, stirring, until it is softened.

2. Add the garlic and continue to sauté, stirring, for 30 seconds.

3. Add the tomatoes and anchovies and cook the mixture over medium-high heat, stirring, for 5 minutes.

4. Add the wine, red pepper flakes, and thyme and bring to a boil, stirring.

5. Reduce the heat to low, add the sea bass, and simmer the bass, covered, for 3 to 4 minutes on each side, or until it is just cooked through.

6. With a slotted spoon transfer the sea bass to a platter and keep it warm, covered.

7. Boil the sauce, stirring, until it is thickened.

8. Add the olives, capers, and salt and pepper to taste, then simmer the sauce for 3 minutes.

9. Spoon the sauce over the bass and sprinkle with the basil. Serve hot or at room temperature.

Shrimp Poached in Beer with Melted Dill Butter

BEER ADDS *a rich flavor to many dishes, especially fish dishes. For what it's worth, I use a nonalcoholic beer in preparing this recipe (Moussy or Kaliber are available just about everywhere these days) because that's what I drink and it doesn't make a bit of difference in the taste. Delicious with whipped potatoes.*

S E R V E S   4

4 tablespoons (½ stick) butter or margarine
2 tablespoons chopped fresh dill leaves
   Salt and pepper
One 12-ounce can beer (regular, light, or
     nonalcoholic)
8 dill sprigs
4 garlic cloves, peeled and minced
1 bay leaf
¼ teaspoon dried thyme
⅛ teaspoon cayenne pepper
1 pound medium-sized shrimp, shelled and
   deveined

1. To make the dill butter, melt the butter in a small saucepan over low heat, add the chopped dill, stir to combine, and season with salt and pepper to taste. Set aside and keep warm.

2. In a large pot, combine the beer, dill sprigs, garlic, bay leaf, thyme, cayenne, and salt and pepper and bring to a boil. Lower the heat and simmer, covered, for 10 minutes.

3. Add the shrimp, return to a boil, and simmer for 1 minute.

4. Remove the shrimp from the pot with a slotted spoon and serve hot, topped with the melted dill butter.

Shrimp in Spicy Tomato Sauce

BECAUSE SHRIMP *is one of the few "fish" high in cholesterol, I'm very careful about how much I eat. When I do decide to fall off the wagon, however, I try to make sure the transgression will be worthwhile. This dish, served over wild rice, certainly fills the bill.*

S E R V E S   4 T O   6

2 pounds shrimp
2 tablespoons butter or margarine
2 tablespoons all-purpose flour
1 cup chopped onion
½ cup canned tomato sauce
2 teaspoons chili powder, or to taste
2 teaspoons sugar
4 teaspoons minced garlic
1 teaspoon Worcestershire sauce
½ teaspoon Angostura bitters
2 tablespoons lemon juice

1. Peel and devein each shrimp, cut down the back with a sharp knife to butterfly, and set aside.

2. Melt butter in a large skillet.

3. Stir in flour and cook over low heat, stirring constantly with a whisk, until the roux begins to turn golden brown.

4. Add the onion and cook the mixture, stirring occasionally, until the onion is softened.

5. Add the tomato sauce, chili powder, sugar, garlic, Worcestershire sauce, bitters and 3 cups hot water and bring the liquid to a boil. Simmer the sauce for 8 to 10 minutes, until it is reduced to about 3 cups.

6. Stir in the shrimp and simmer them for 1 to 2 minutes, until they are just firm.

7. Stir in lemon juice and serve hot.

Shrimp with Cabbage and Caviar

ANOTHER RECIPE that looks and tastes as absolutely marvelous as it sounds. And no need to bother with Beluga caviar—the inexpensive lumpfish caviar is just fine.

S E R V E S   4   T O   6

2 cups White Fish Stock (page 258)
40 shrimp (about 2 pounds), shelled, reserving the shells
1 large shallot, peeled and finely chopped
¼ cup dry white wine
2 tablespoons dry vermouth
1 cup cream or half-and-half
Salt and pepper
1 tablespoon vegetable oil
1 pound cabbage, sliced thin
4 teaspoons black lumpfish caviar
4 teaspoons red lumpfish caviar

1. In a large saucepan, combine the stock, the shrimp shells, the shallot, the wine, and the vermouth, bring the liquid to a boil, and boil for 8 minutes.

2. Add the cream and boil the mixture for about 20 minutes, or until it is reduced to about 1 cup.

3. Strain the sauce through a fine sieve into a small saucepan, season to taste with salt and pepper, and keep it warm, covered, over very low heat.

4. In another large saucepan, heat the vegetable oil and sauté the cabbage, covered, over medium heat, stirring occasionally, for 5 minutes, or until it is just beginning to get tender (al dente).

5. Over a pot of boiling water, steam the shrimp for 1 or 2 minutes until just firm.

6. Spoon the vermouth sauce onto warm dinner plates, arrange the shrimp around the edges of the plates, and divide the cabbage among the plates, mounding it in the center.

7. Top the cabbage with the black caviar and sprinkle the red caviar over the shrimp. Serve hot or at room temperature.

Poached Skate with Cilantro Vinaigrette

A VERY simple but effective way to bring out all the subtle flavors of the skate. Try serving this dish at room temperature.

S E R V E S 4

2 pounds trimmed skate wings, cut into 4 equal pieces
1 onion, peeled and sliced
2 sprigs parsley
2 tablespoons white wine vinegar

THE CILANTRO VINAIGRETTE

2 tablespoons sherry vinegar
1 teaspoon Dijon-style mustard
2 tablespoons vegetable oil
¼ cup olive oil
2 tablespoons chopped fresh cilantro
1 tablespoon sliced scallion greens
1 small red onion, peeled and thinly sliced
Salt and pepper

Lettuce
Tomato and cucumber slices

1. In a shallow pan, place the skate, onion, parsley, and white wine vinegar, and add enough water to cover. Bring to a simmer and cook for 15 minutes. With a slotted spatula, transfer skate to a plate and refrigerate.

2. To make the vinaigrette, whisk together in a bowl the sherry vinegar and mustard. Combine the oils and add, whisking continuously.

. . .

163

3. Stir in the cilantro, scallion greens, and red onion slices, and season to taste with salt and pepper.

4. Line 4 plates with lettuce, place skate on lettuce, drizzle with vinaigrette, and garnish with tomato and cucumber slices. Serve cold or at room temperature.

Poached Skate in Sauce Gribiche

THIS CLASSIC *French sauce is perfect with skate, and many other dishes as well. You may substitute diced sour pickles for the cornichons and you'll hardly tell the difference.*

S E R V E S   4

1 tablespoon plus 1 teaspoon red wine vinegar
1 tablespoon plus 1 teaspoon dry sherry
2 tablespoons plus 2 teaspoons olive oil
1 tablespoon plus 1 teaspoon vegetable oil
¼ cup diced red onion
2 tablespoons diced cornichons
  (small French pickles)
1½ teaspoons drained capers
½ teaspoon Dijon-style mustard
Salt and pepper
4 cups Court Bouillon (page 257)
2 pounds trimmed skate wing
2 hard-boiled eggs, yolks and whites minced
  separately
¼ cup minced fresh parsley leaves

1. In a bowl, whisk together the vinegar, the sherry, and the oils, whisking until the mixture is emulsified.

2. Add the onion, cornichons, capers, and mustard and mix well. Season to taste with salt and pepper and set aside.

3. In a large saucepan, bring the court bouillon to a boil over high heat and put in the skate wing. Reduce the heat to medium and simmer for 6 to 8 minutes, or until the skate wing is opaque.

4. Remove the skate from the bouillon and cut it into 4 equal pieces. Arrange it on 4 plates.

5. Pour equal amounts of the sauce gribiche over the skate and garnish each piece with egg yolk, egg white, and parsley. Serve hot.

Sole with Lemon-Ginger Sauce and Fried Leeks

THIS IS *actually two recipes in one—the fried leeks can be used to accompany any number of other dishes. Crunchy steamed baby carrots make a good accompaniment.*

S E R V E S 4

2 large leeks, trimmed, leaving ½ inch of the green part
1½ cups vegetable oil for deep-frying
¼ cup minced shallot
4 teaspoons peeled grated fresh gingerroot
4 tablespoons (½ stick) butter or margarine
1 cup dry white wine
1 teaspoon salt
4 sole fillets, 6 to 8 ounces each
2 teaspoons cornstarch
2 tablespoons fresh lemon juice
2 egg yolks

1. Remove the 2 outer leaves of each leek. Slice these 4 leaves crosswise, reserving the inner parts of the leeks for another use. Wash the sliced leek and pat it dry.

2. In a skillet, heat the vegetable oil and fry the sliced leek until lightly browned. Transfer it with a slotted spoon to a paper towel to drain, and keep warm in a 200-degree oven.

3. In a saucepan, combine the shallot, gingeroot, butter, wine, salt, and 1 cup water, bring the mixture to a boil, and boil for 10 minutes.

4. In a skillet, arrange the sole fillets in one layer. Strain the wine mixture through a sieve over the sole and poach the sole at a simmer, turning it once, for 3 minutes, or until it just flakes.

5. Remove the sole from the heat and let stand, covered. Drain the poaching liquid into a saucepan.

6. Boil the poaching liquid until it is reduced to about ½ cup.

7. In a bowl, whisk together the cornstarch and lemon juice, add the mixture to the boiling liquid, whisking constantly, and simmer the mixture for 2 minutes.

8. In another bowl, whisk together the egg yolks and 1 teaspoon water. Add half the hot liquid, whisking, and whisk the mixture back into the remaining hot liquid. Cook the sauce over moderate heat, stirring, until it is thick enough to coat the spoon; do not let it boil.

9. Transfer the sole to 4 warmed plates, cover each fillet with sauce, and top each with a mound of fried leek. Serve hot.

Tuna with Forty Garlic Cloves

YOU'VE PROBABLY *seen the chicken version of this recipe, a classic French creation. I have no idea why we use forty cloves instead of thirty-nine or forty-one, but I guess it makes a nice round number—and a most savory dish.*

S E R V E S   4

2   tablespoons butter or margarine
¼   cup olive oil
40 large cloves garlic, unpeeled
1   cup dry white wine
4   tuna steaks, 6 to 8 ounces each
    Salt and pepper
½   cup minced fresh parsley leaves

1. In a large skillet, melt the butter with the oil over medium-high heat. Add the 40 cloves of garlic, stir, cover the skillet and cook for 10 minutes, stirring occasionally.

2. Add the wine and stir, scraping up any brown bits from the bottom of the skillet.

3. Season the tuna steaks with salt and pepper to taste, add them to the skillet with the garlic, and cook the tuna, turning once, for about 6 minutes (the steaks will be rare inside, but that's the best way to eat tuna).

4. Remove the tuna steaks from the skillet with a slotted spatula and put them on a platter, covered, to keep them warm.

5. Continue simmering the sauce for another 5 minutes, until it is reduced by about half.

6. Pour the sauce and garlic on the tuna and sprinkle with parsley. Serve hot.

Entrées

Baked

Baked Bluefish with Farmer Cheese, Yogurt, and Mint

HERE'S A *low-calorie, tangy sauce that goes perfectly with the rich, distinctive taste of bluefish.*

S E R V E S   4

¼   cup olive oil
2   medium zucchini, thinly sliced
3   cups peeled, seeded, and chopped tomatoes
2   cups farmer or hoop cheese
6   tablespoons plain yogurt
½   cup chopped fresh mint, or 2 tablespoons dried mint
4   bluefish fillets, 6 to 8 ounces each

1. In a saucepan, heat the oil and sauté the zucchini for 3 minutes over medium heat.

2. Add the tomatoes and cook 2 minutes more.

3. Spread the mixture in a baking dish large enough to hold the bluefish fillets. Preheat the oven to 400 degrees.

4. In a bowl, combine the farmer cheese, yogurt, and mint and dip each bluefish fillet in the mixture until each is coated.

5. Lay the bluefish fillets on top of the vegetable mixture in the baking pan, spread the remainder of the farmer cheese mixture on top of the fillets, and bake for 12 to 15 minutes, or until the fish just flakes.

6. Serve hot from the baking dish.

Whole Baked Bluefish with Raisins and Rice

I DON'T do whole fishes very often, but when I find a nice, fresh bluefish, I like to do it this way. The already flavorful stuffing becomes downright delectable when enhanced by the oils of the bluefish.

S E R V E S   6

3 tablespoons olive oil
1 cup minced onion
½ cup whole pine nuts
1 cup raw long-grain rice
2½ cups White Fish Stock (page 258)
Freshly ground black pepper
½ teaspoon cinnamon
¼ teaspoon nutmeg
½ cup raisins, soaked in water for 30 minutes and drained
½ cup chopped fresh parsley leaves
One 5-pound whole bluefish, gutted, scaled, gills and center backbone removed by your fishmonger, with head and tail intact

1. In a large saucepan, heat the oil and sauté the onion until translucent.

2. Add the pine nuts and rice, and sauté until the rice is shiny, 2 or 3 minutes.

3. Add fish stock, black pepper, cinnamon, and nutmeg, and bring the liquid to a boil.

4. Lower heat to simmer, cover, and cook until the rice absorbs the liquid, about 10 to 12 minutes.

5. Stir in raisins and chopped parsley, and remove from heat.

6. Preheat oven to 400 degrees.

7. Spoon the rice stuffing into the body cavity of the bluefish, secure with twine, and bake in an ovenproof dish for 20 to 30 minutes. Serve hot.

Baked Bluefish with Sour Cream and Tomato Sauce

I'VE TRIED *this sauce with other fish, but this very simple tomato mixture seems to bring out the best in bluefish. Serve it with a spinach pasta tossed with garlic and oil.*

S E R V E S 4

One	14 ½-ounce can plum tomatoes, including the juice
4	bluefish fillets, about 6 to 8 ounces each
⅓	cup sour cream
4	fresh plum tomatoes, thinly sliced
1	yellow bell pepper, seeded and cut into thin rings
1	red bell pepper, seeded and cut into thin rings
1	green bell pepper, seeded and cut into thin rings
	Salt and white pepper
	Minced fresh parsley leaves

1. In a saucepan, bring the canned tomatoes and their juice to a boil and simmer the mixture, stirring occasionally, for 10 to 12 minutes. Meanwhile, preheat the oven to 400 degrees.

2. In a blender or food processor fitted with the steel blade, purée the tomato mixture.

3. Pour the sauce into a large baking dish and add the bluefish fillets in one layer.

4. Spread the sour cream over the top of the bluefish, then top the sour cream with the fresh tomato slices and the yellow, red, and green pepper rings, overlapping them. Season with salt and white pepper to taste.

5. Bake the mixture for 10 to 12 minutes, or until the bluefish just flakes.

6. Transfer equal portions to each of 4 warm plates and sprinkle with parsley. Serve hot.

Catfish Fillets with Sesame Seeds

SESAME ADDS *a distinctive flavor to any dish, although you might want to use a little less sesame oil than the recipe calls for. The first time I ever cooked this dish I heated up some leftover spaghetti squash to go with it. Perfecto!*

S E R V E S   4

1   cup breadcrumbs
⅓   cup sesame seeds
1   tablespoon minced fresh parsley leaves
4   catfish fillets, 6 to 8 ounces each
      All-purpose flour
2   eggs, lightly beaten
3   tablespoons vegetable oil
3   tablespoons sesame oil

1. Preheat the oven to 350 degrees.

2. In a shallow dish, stir together the breadcrumbs, sesame seeds, and parsley.

3. Dredge the catfish fillets in the flour, shaking off the excess. Then dip them in the eggs, and coat them with the crumb mixture.

4. In a large skillet with an ovenproof handle, heat the vegetable oil and 1 tablespoon of the sesame oil over medium-high heat and sauté the fillets, turning them once, for 1 minute, or until they are golden.

5. Transfer the skillet to the preheated oven. Bake the fillets for 12 to 15 minutes, or until they are cooked through, and arrange them on a heated platter over a bed of braised spinach.

6. In a small saucepan, heat the remaining 2 tablespoons of sesame oil and drizzle it over the catfish. Serve hot.

Codfish Loaf with Herbed Butter Sauce

THIS IS *a delicious substitute for meatloaf. Not a fancy dish, but a real stick-to-the-ribs wintertime treat.*

S E R V E S   4

3   tablespoons butter or margarine
½   cup minced scallions
3   tablespoons all-purpose flour
1   cup milk, scalded
⅛   teaspoon cayenne pepper
2   carrots, peeled and cut into julienne strips
½   pound green beans, trimmed
2   pounds cod fillets, cut into 1-inch pieces
4   egg whites (reserve yolks for another use)
    Salt and pepper
    Dill sprigs
    Herbed Butter Sauce (Page 247)

1. In a saucepan, melt the butter over medium heat and sauté the scallions until they're soft.

2. Stir in flour and cook the roux for 2 minutes, whisking constantly.

3. Add scalded milk, whisking until the mixture is blended. Add cayenne and cook the sauce over low heat until it is thickened. Set aside to cool.

4. Blanch julienned carrots in boiling water for 2 minutes, drain, rinse under cold water, and reserve.

5. Blanch beans in boiling water for 3 minutes, drain, rinse under cold water, and reserve.

6. In a food processor fitted with the steel blade, purée the cod pieces and the egg whites.

Entrées

· · ·

175

7. Add ¾ of the cooled sauce and blend, then add salt and pepper to taste.

8. Preheat the oven to 400 degrees.

9. Spoon ⅓ of the fish mixture into a greased glass 1½-quart loaf pan. Smooth the top with a spatula and arrange half the blanched beans lengthwise. Cover the beans with the remaining sauce and arrange all of the carrots on top. Cover with another ⅓ of the fish mixture, then arrange the remaining beans on top. Add the remaining ⅓ of the fish mixture. Allow to settle.

10. Put loaf pan in a larger baking pan and add enough hot water to reach halfway up the loaf pan. Cover top of loaf with a buttered piece of wax paper, and bake the ensemble for 1 hour, or until a knife inserted in the center comes out clean.

11. Carefully remove from oven and remove loaf pan from water bath. Allow to cool, then run a sharp knife around the edges of the loaf pan, place a platter on top of the pan, and invert the loaf to the center of the platter.

12. Place the loaf back in the oven for 10 minutes, or until it's hot.

13. Garnish with sprigs of fresh dill and serve hot with herbed butter sauce.

Flounder Stuffed with Mushrooms with Tarragon Sauce

SOMETIMES, IN putting together a recipe, a surprise ingredient will make the difference between a good dish and an excellent one. In this case, I decided to add a little port wine, which had been brought to me by one of my dinner guests. The result was memorable.

SERVES 6

1 pound mushrooms, cleaned and coarsely chopped
3 tablespoons butter or margarine
4 shallots, peeled and minced
1 tablespoon dried tarragon
¼ cup port wine
⅓ cup cream or half-and-half
2 tablespoons all-purpose flour
   Salt and pepper
6 flounder fillets, 6 to 8 ounces each
½ cup dry white wine
   Tarragon Sauce (page 249)

1. Mince the mushrooms in a blender or food processor fitted with the steel blade.

2. In a large skillet, melt the butter over medium heat, add the shallots and tarragon, and sauté for 5 minutes.

3. Stir in the mushrooms and sauté over medium heat for 3 minutes, or until the mushrooms begin to exude juice.

4. Add port and cream, increase heat, and cook for about 10 minutes, or until the mixture is reduced by about half.

5. Add flour and stir over low heat until well blended.

6. Season to taste with salt and pepper, transfer to a bowl, and refrigerate until ready to use.

7. Preheat the oven to 400 degrees.

8. Place 1 or 2 tablespoons of the mushroom stuffing on each flounder fillet and roll up crosswise. Place rolled fillets side by side in a buttered baking dish.

9. Combine wine with ½ cup water and pour over the fish.

10. Cover the dish with foil and bake for 15 minutes, or until the fish just flakes.

11. Serve hot with tarragon sauce.

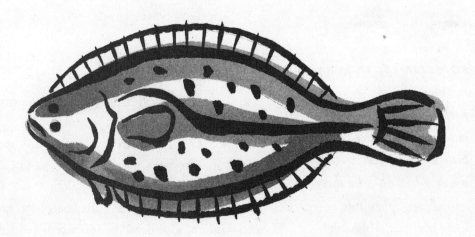

Baked Haddock Fillets in Mornay Sauce

CHEESE AND *fish don't usually go together (except for smoked fish, like lox and cream cheese, or whitefish and cream cheese.) But haddock and other members of the cod family are very compatible with a classic mornay sauce.*

S E R V E S 4

1 cup Sauce Mornay (page 245)
2 tablespoons dry sherry
1 tablespoon fennel seeds
4 haddock fillets, 6 to 8 ounces each
   Chopped fresh parsley leaves

1. Preheat the oven to 425 degrees.

2. Prepare the mornay sauce and add to it the sherry and fennel seeds.

3. Place the haddock fillets in a greased baking dish, and pour the sauce over them.

4. Bake the fish for 6 to 8 minutes, or until it just flakes.

5. Transfer the fillets to 4 warm dinner plates, spoon the sauce over each, and sprinkle with chopped parsley. Serve hot.

Halibut Fillets with Anisette and Fennel

THIS RECIPE *is just as delicious using sea bass, grouper, or monkfish.*

S E R V E S 4

1   tablespoon olive oil
4   halibut fillets, about 6 to 8 ounces each
    Salt and pepper
½   cup anisette
2   navel oranges, peeled and sliced, each slice cut into quarters
2   large fennel bulbs, peeled and sliced, crosswise, each slice cut into quarters
2   large red onions, halved lengthwise and thinly sliced
1   cup fennel greens, finely chopped

1. Preheat the oven to 400 degrees.

2. Grease a baking dish with the olive oil and add the halibut fillets. Season with salt and pepper to taste and sprinkle with anisette.

3. In a bowl, mix together the orange nuggets, quartered fennel, and red onion slices and scatter evenly over the fillets.

4. Bake the fillets and vegetables for about 12 to 15 minutes, until the fillets are just cooked through.

5. Transfer the fillets and the vegetable mixture to a serving platter and sprinkle with the fennel greens. Serve hot.

Baked Mackerel with Three-Pepper Sauce

A THING *of beauty is a joy forever—and properly prepared and presented this dish more than does justice to the somewhat lowly mackerel, both in looks and in taste.*

S E R V E S   6

¼ cup olive oil
1 tablespoon chopped garlic
2 onions, peeled and finely chopped
1 cup sliced red bell pepper
1 cup sliced yellow bell pepper
1 cup sliced green bell pepper
½ teaspoon dried thyme
1 bay leaf
¼ teaspoon Tabasco sauce
3 cups crushed Italian canned tomatoes
   Salt and pepper
12 mackerel fillets (about 2 pounds total weight)

1. Preheat the oven to 425 degrees.

2. In a frying pan heat 3 tablespoons of the olive oil over medium-high heat and add the garlic and onion. Sauté until the onion is wilted.

3. Add the red, yellow, and green peppers and continue cooking, stirring occasionally, until the onions start to brown slightly.

4. Add the thyme, bay leaf, Tabasco sauce, tomatoes, and salt and pepper to taste and cook, stirring occasionally, for 7 minutes.

5. Coat a baking dish with the remaining 1 tablespoon of olive oil and arrange the mackerel fillets side by side in the dish. Pour the sauce over them and bake for 15 minutes, or until the fish just flakes.

6. Transfer the fillets to individual plates and top each one with sauce. Serve hot.

Stuffed Mussels

PREPARE THE mussels according to recipe for Mussels à la Marinière (page 138). Save the broth. Remove the mussels from the shells, but keep the half shells. Chop the mussel meat coarsely and combine with the stuffing.

SERVES 4

6   tablespoons (¾ stick) butter or margarine
¼   cup chopped onion
3   tablespoons chopped celery
1   tablespoon chopped green bell pepper
¼   cup chopped fresh parsley leaves
1   cup toasted breadcrumbs
1   teaspoon dry mustard
1   teaspoon salt
⅛   teaspoon cayenne pepper
24 cooked mussels, chopped

1. Preheat the oven to 450 degrees.

2. In a large saucepan, melt 4 tablespoons (½ stick) of the butter over medium-high heat and sauté the onion, celery, and green pepper until just tender.

3. Add the parsley, breadcrumbs, dry mustard, salt, and cayenne pepper, and stir until the mixture is blended.

4. Add the chopped mussels and a few tablespoons of the broth reserved from steaming and stir until you have a moist, but thick, mixture. Spoon this into the half shells and dot with remaining butter.

5. Place the stuffed shells in a baking dish and bake until they are lightly browned. Serve hot.

Baked Orange Roughy with Artichoke-Lemon and Mint Sauce

THIS RECIPE *was born because I happened to have been given a big bag of fresh mint, and I was planning on cooking orange roughy for dinner. Serve with mashed sweet potatoes with pineapple chunks.*

S E R V E S   6

½ cup drained bottled marinated artichoke hearts
2 tablespoons drained capers
2 tablespoons chopped fresh mint leaves or 1 teaspoon dried mint
2 garlic cloves, peeled and coarsely chopped
1 egg yolk
2 tablespoons fresh lemon juice
¼ cup plus 2 tablespoons olive oil
Salt and pepper
6 orange roughy fillets, 6 to 8 ounces each
6 sprigs fresh mint
6 thin lemon slices, quartered

1. Preheat the oven to 450 degrees.

2. In a blender or food processor fitted with the steel blade, purée the artichoke hearts, capers, chopped mint, garlic, egg yolk, and lemon juice. With the motor running, add ¼ cup olive oil in a stream, blending until the sauce is smooth. Add salt and pepper to taste and pulse once or twice.

3. Rub the orange roughy fillets with the remaining 2 tablespoons olive oil, wrap each fillet in foil, and bake on a baking sheet for 8 minutes, or until the fish just flakes.

4. Unwrap the packets and with a slotted spoon transfer each fillet to a hot plate.

5. Spoon the sauce around the fillets and garnish them with the mint sprigs and lemon slices. Serve hot.

Baked Pompano in Red Wine Sauce

POMPANO IS *a fine, subtle fish that tastes great plain. But this delicate wine sauce is perfect with this most delicate fish. You can prepare this dish without the arrowroot (eliminate step 7) which will give you a much thinner but just as tasty sauce.*

S E R V E S   4

6   tablespoons (¾ stick) butter or margarine
3   tablespoons finely chopped shallots
4   pompano fillets, about 6 to 8 ounces each
    Salt and pepper
1   cup dry red wine, preferably Cabernet
    Sauvignon
½   cup White Fish Stock (page 258)
1   tablespoon arrowroot

1. Preheat the oven to 425 degrees. Rub a baking pan with 2 tablespoons of the butter and sprinkle the shallots over it.

2. Arrange the fillets in one layer in the pan and season to taste with salt and pepper.

3. Add the wine and fish broth and dot the fillets with 1 tablespoon of the butter.

4. Place the baking pan in the preheated oven and bake for 5 to 7 minutes, or until the fish just flakes.

5. Remove the pan from the oven, transfer the fillets with a slotted spatula to a warm platter, and cover with foil to keep them warm.

6. Pour the cooking liquid and shallots into a saucepan, and cook over high heat until the mixture is reduced to about 1 cup.

7. Combine 1 tablespoon of butter with the arrowroot, blending well with your fingers, then stir this into the wine mixture. Bring to a boil, stirring, then strain the mixture through a sieve and return to the saucepan.

8. Swirl in the remaining 2 tablespoons of butter and heat until it melts, then pour the sauce over the fillets. Serve hot.

Baked Red Snapper with Eggplant, Basil, and Coriander

HERE'S A *case of using a pasta sauce to complement a piece of fish. I had made the eggplant and basil sauce many times for pasta, and one night, as I pondered what to do with a couple of snapper fillets, I noticed I had some of that delicious sauce sitting in my refrigerator. Necessity being the mother of invention (I needed to use the sauce), I poured it over the fish, baked it, and the rest, as they say, is history.*

S E R V E S 4

4 red snapper fillets, about 6 to 8 ounces each
   Salt and pepper
1 medium-sized eggplant (about 1 pound)
5 tablespoons olive oil
1½ cups thinly sliced onion
2 teaspoons chopped garlic
1 cup peeled, seeded, and chopped tomatoes
1 tablespoon freshly grated gingerroot
1 cup dry white wine
¼ cup chopped fresh coriander leaves
¼ cup chopped fresh basil leaves
¼ cup fresh lime juice

Preheat the oven to 425 degrees.

1. Season the snapper fillets with salt and pepper to taste and set aside.

2. Peel the eggplant and cut into ¼-inch cubes

3. In a saucepan, heat ¼ cup of the olive oil over medium-high heat. Add the onion and garlic and sauté, stirring, until the onion is translucent but not browned.

4. Add the eggplant and stir. Then add the tomatoes and cook, stirring, for 2 minutes.

5. Stir in the ginger, add wine, coriander, basil, lime juice, and salt and pepper to taste, bring the mixture to a boil, and then reduce the heat and simmer for 10 minutes.

6. Pour the remaining 1 tablespoon of olive oil into a baking dish large enough to hold the fillets in one layer and arrange the fillets in the dish. Spoon some sauce over them and bake for about 10 minutes.

7. Remove the fillets to individual plates and serve hot, with the remaining sauce on the side.

Red Snapper with Sake and Black Bean Sauce

WHEN I *lived in New York, there was a lovely fish restaurant called Wilkinson's around the corner from our apartment. It was a "special occasion" place, but my wife and I invented many a special occasion as an excuse to go. Of all the dishes I tried there, this was my favorite. And they always served it with a little mound of crisp julienned vegetables and a potato of some kind.*

S E R V E S   6

Dry white wine
6   red snapper fillets, about 6 to 8 ounces each
1   cup sake
3   tablespoons dried black beans, rinsed in a sieve
    to remove salt
3   tablespoons finely chopped shallots
2   tablespoons finely grated fresh gingerroot
4   teaspoons soy sauce
2   tablespoons sesame oil
1½ cups Beurre Blanc (page 246)
12 peeled orange segments

1. Preheat the oven to 400 degrees.

2. Pour the wine into a baking dish to a depth of about ¼ inch and lay the fillets in the wine. Bake them for 10 to 12 minutes, or until they just flake.

3. In a sauté pan, combine the sake, black beans, shallots, gingerroot, soy sauce, and sesame oil and cook over medium-high heat until the mixture is reduced so the contents of the pan are nearly dry. Remove from heat.

4. Remove the red snapper fillets from the oven and place them on a warm platter or individual plates.

5. Add the beurre blanc to the sake mixture, stir thoroughly, and pour the sauce beside each fillet. Arrange 2 orange segments at the tail end of each fillet. Serve hot.

Baked Sea Bass with Brandy and Orange Sauce

YOU CAN *substitute orange juice for the Curaçao in this recipe, but if you do, increase the amount of brandy from one tablespoon to three for approximately the same eventual flavor.*

S E R V E S   4

¼ cup Curaçao (orange-flavored liqueur)

2 tablespoons dry sherry

4 sea bass fillets, 6 to 8 ounces each

2 tablespoons butter or margarine

½ teaspoon dried tarragon, crumbled

1 tablespoon brandy

½ cup orange juice

⅓ cup Beurre Blanc (page 246)

Orange slices

Parsley sprigs

1. Preheat the oven to 400 degrees.

2. In a small bowl combine 2 tablespoons Curaçao, the sherry, and 2 tablespoons water.

3. Place the sea bass fillets in a baking dish in one layer, pour the sherry mixture over them, and dot the fillets with 1 tablespoon of the butter.

4. Bake the sea bass for 10 to 12 minutes, or until it just flakes. Remove the baking dish from the oven and cover with foil to keep warm.

5. In a small saucepan, combine the remaining Curaçao, the remaining 1 tablespoon butter, the tarragon, brandy, and orange juice, bring the liquid to a boil, then reduce the heat and simmer for 3 minutes. Remove the saucepan from the heat and whisk in the beurre blanc.

6. Transfer the sea bass fillets to warm plates, spoon the brandy orange sauce over each fillet, and garnish with orange slices and parsley. Serve hot.

Baked Sea Bass with Goat Cheese and Pernod

WHEN *I first saw this dish listed on the menu of a hotel dining room in Detroit, I laughed out loud. Talk about pretentious titles—this was something I'd expect to find in a trendy place on one of the coasts. But I was curious, so I ordered it and was I pleasantly surprised. I brought the recipe home and have served it three or four times to friends. Who all laughed when I told them what it was called.*

S E R V E S   6

6	tablespoons olive oil
½	cup chopped onion
1	tablespoon finely chopped garlic
½	cup dry white wine
3	cups canned crushed tomatoes
2	tablespoons drained capers
½	teaspoon dried rosemary
½	teaspoon dried oregano
¼	teaspoon hot red pepper flakes
	Salt and pepper
½	cup chopped fresh parsley leaves
6	sea bass fillets, about 6 to 8 ounces each
2	tablespoons Pernod or anisette
½	pound mild goat cheese, crumbled

1. In a saucepan, heat 3 tablespoons of the olive oil, then add the onion and garlic and cook, stirring occasionally, until the onion is just beginning to soften. (Do not let the garlic brown.)

2. Add the wine, tomatoes, capers, rosemary, oregano, hot pepper flakes, and salt and pepper to taste, and the parsley. Bring to a boil and then lower the heat and simmer the mixture for about 10 minutes. Preheat the oven to 425 degrees.

3. Pour the remaining 3 tablespoons of olive oil into a baking dish large enough to hold the fillets in one layer, and arrange the sea bass on the oil.

4. Pour the tomato sauce over the fillets and bake for 8 to 10 minutes.

5. Sprinkle the Pernod over the fish and sauce and top with the crumbled goat cheese.

6. Bake for 3 minutes longer, then remove the fillets to individual plates and spoon the Pernod, cheese, and tomato mixture over each fillet. Serve hot.

Sea Bass Fillets in Parchment Packets

FOIL PACKETS *may be substituted, but there's something just a bit more elegant about parchment.*

S E R V E S 4

4 sea bass fillets, 6 to 8 ounces each
2 teaspoons chili paste with soy bean (available in better supermarkets and Asian specialty stores)
4 teaspoons sesame oil
1 white onion, peeled and thinly sliced
2 teaspoons minced fresh gingerroot
2 teaspoons soy sauce

1. Cut four 12-inch squares of parchment or foil. Place a sea bass fillet at one end of each piece of parchment or foil. Preheat the oven to 450 degrees.

2. Rub ½ teaspoon of the chili paste into each fillet and pour 1 teaspoon of sesame oil over each.

3. Divide the sliced onions among the fillets.

4. Sprinkle each with ½ teaspoon gingerroot and ½ teaspoon soy sauce.

5. Close the parchment or foil over the fillets and fold the ends in; continue to wrap, finally making a very narrow fold and crimping the edges to insure that the packets are tightly sealed.

6. Place the packets on a baking sheet and bake for 7 minutes. Remove from the oven and let sit for another 2 minutes.

7. Serve the packets on individual plates and invite your guests to slit the packets open and remove the piping hot fish.

Sole Stuffed with Crabmeat

THIS WAS *one of the first "fancy" fish dishes I ever cooked. I remember thinking it was the fishy equivalent of those ancient dinner party favorites, beef tournedos. There is something frankly old-fashioned about this recipe—and what's wrong with that? To complete the picture, serve this with sautéed spinach and onions.*

S E R V E S   6

2 cups lump crabmeat, picked over
1 egg, lightly beaten
½ cup chopped scallions
2 tablespoons Dijon-style mustard
¼ cup fine fresh breadcrumbs
½ cup chopped fresh parsley leaves
   Salt and pepper
12 sole fillets (about 3 pounds)
2 tablespoons chopped shallots
3 tablespoons butter or margarine, melted
1 cup dry white wine

1. Preheat the oven to 425 degrees.

2. In a mixing bowl, combine the crab, egg, scallions, mustard, breadcrumbs, parsley, and salt and pepper to taste and blend well.

3. Place equal amounts of the stuffing on six of the flounder fillets, leaving a small margin all around. Fit the other six fillets on top of the filling and press down lightly.

4. Arrange the stuffed fillets in one layer in a greased baking pan, and sprinkle the chopped shallots around the fish.

5. Brush the melted butter over the fillets and pour the wine into the baking pan.

6. Bake for 8 to 10 minutes, or until the fish just flakes.

7. Remove the fillets to a serving platter and pour the juices from the baking pan over them. Serve hot.

Sole with Macadamia Nut Sauce

AN ELEGANT *entrée.
The subtle flavor of the
sole accented by unique
taste of the macadamia
nuts gives an air of real
distinction to this
serve-to-your-company dish.
Steamed, crisp, fresh green
beans are a perfect
accompaniment.*

S E R V E S   4

1	tablespoon butter or margarine
3	tablespoons chopped shallots
½	cup dry white wine
¾	cup cream or half-and-half
1½	cup whole roasted macadamia nuts
4	sole fillets, about 6 to 8 ounces each
½	teaspoon fresh lemon juice
	Salt and pepper
2	tablespoons minced fresh parsley leaves

1. Melt the butter in a large saucepan and add the shallots. Sauté over low heat, stirring, until the shallots are softened.

2. Add ¼ cup of the wine, then stir in the cream, bring the mixture to a boil, and simmer, stirring, for 1 or 2 minutes until the mixture is thickened.

3. Remove the pan from the heat and let the mixture cool.

4. Preheat the oven to 400 degrees.

5. Grind 1 cup of the macadamia nuts in a blender or food processor fitted with the steel blade, then add the cooled cream mixture and blend the sauce until it is smooth. Transfer to a bowl and cover with aluminum foil or plastic wrap.

6. Place the sole fillets in a buttered baking dish in 1 layer. Add the remaining ¼ cup wine and bake for about 7 to 8 minutes, or until the fillets flake.

Entrées

. . .

7. Transfer fillets to a heated platter, reserving the cooking liquid, and cover with aluminum foil to keep them warm.

8. Remove cover from sauce and whisk in 2 tablespoons of the cooking liquid, the lemon juice, and salt and pepper to taste.

9. Spoon the sauce over the fillets and sprinkle them with the parsley and the remaining ½ cup of macadamia nuts, coarsely chopped. Serve hot.

Baked Striped Bass Fillets with Caviar Butter

CAVIAR BUTTER *is just one of several butter spreads that goes wonderfully well with just about any fish. You do not need to buy expensive caviar—feel free to use black or red lumpfish caviar or red salmon roe.*

S E R V E S   4

T H E   C A V I A R   B U T T E R

¼ cup caviar

8 tablespoons (1 stick) butter or margarine, softened

4 striped bass fillets, 6 to 8 ounces each

¼ cup vegetable oil

¼ cup wine

1. To make the caviar butter, blend the caviar and butter in a blender or food processor fitted with the steel blade.

2. Preheat the oven to 425 degrees.

3. Rub the striped bass fillets with oil.

4. Pour the wine and ¼ cup water into a baking dish, and arrange the fillets in the pan.

5. Bake the bass for 6 to 8 minutes, or until the fish just flakes.

6. Remove from the oven and transfer the fillets to 4 warm dinner plates with a slotted spatula. Spoon the caviar butter over each fillet and serve hot, as the butter just begins to melt.

Entrées

Striped Bass and Shrimp Casserole

ANOTHER CONCOCTION *from my favorite cousin. Neil loves "strip-ed" bass, as he is wont to call them, and he also makes casseroles, which I don't do a lot of. One night when he made this, I took his recipe home, along with a huge bowl of leftovers—and have made it several times over the years.*

SERVES 4

3   tablespoons olive oil
2   onions, peeled and chopped
2   green bell peppers, seeded and chopped
1   clove garlic, peeled and minced
1/8   teaspoon cayenne pepper, or to taste
2   tomatoes, peeled and diced
1   tablespoon minced fresh cilantro
2   pounds striped bass fillets, cut into 1-inch strips
1   pound medium shrimp (about 24), shelled and deveined

1. Preheat the oven to 425 degrees.

2. In a saucepan, heat the olive oil on medium-high heat, then sauté the onions, green peppers, garlic, and cayenne until all the vegetables are tender. Remove from heat and mix in the tomatoes and cilantro.

3. In a greased casserole dish, layer the fish and shrimp with the vegetable mixture, alternating layers until everything is used.

4. Cover casserole and bake for 15 to 20 minutes. Serve hot.

Baked Swordfish with Carrot and Fennel

S E R V E S   4

2 tablespoons olive oil
2 large carrots, peeled and cut into julienne strips
2 small fennel bulbs (about ½ pound), trimmed and cut into julienne strips
2 teaspoons freshly grated orange rind
¼ cup dry white wine
4 teaspoons fresh lemon juice
 Salt and white pepper
4 swordfish steaks, 6 to 8 ounces each

1. Preheat the oven to 450 degrees.

2. Heat the olive oil in a large skillet and sauté the carrot and fennel strips over medium heat for 5 or 6 minutes, stirring occasionally.

3. Add the orange rind, wine, and lemon juice and cook, stirring, for 1 to 2 minutes, until the liquid is reduced slightly. Add salt and white pepper to taste, and cook the mixture another 1 to 2 minutes.

4. Place each swordfish steak on a large piece of aluminum foil, top each with some of the vegetable mixture, then fold the foil around snugly to make 4 tightly sealed packets.

5. Place the packets on a baking sheet or in a baking pan and bake for 10 to 12 minutes. Open a packet and

Entrées

check to make sure the swordfish is done. (There should be no pink in the center.)

6. Remove the packets from the oven, open each one and transfer the swordfish and vegetable mixture to 4 heated plates. Serve hot.

Baked Tilefish with Filberts and Cheddar

THIS RECIPE *is also delicious with catfish.*

S E R V E S   4

4   tilefish steaks or fillets, 6 to 8 ounces each
    Salt and pepper
    Juice of 1 lime
1   cup shelled filberts (hazelnuts), blanched
4   tablespoons (½ stick) butter or margarine
3   tablespoons milk
¼   cup dry sherry
1   cup grated sharp Cheddar cheese
½   cup breadcrumbs
⅛   teaspoon nutmeg

1. Season the tilefish with salt and pepper to taste, sprinkle with lime juice, and set aside for 1 hour.

2. In a skillet, roast the filberts in 2 tablespoons of the butter until they turn slightly golden, remove them from the skillet with a slotted spoon, then purée them in a food processor fitted with the steel blade to a pasty powder.

3. Mix the ground nuts in a bowl with the milk and sherry, then stir in the cheese.

4. Preheat the oven to 425 degrees.

5. In a saucepan, melt the remaining 2 tablespoons of butter and stir in the breadcrumbs.

6. Place the tilefish fillets in a greased baking pan and spread the nut-cheese mixture over them.

7. Sprinkle the tilefish with the buttered crumbs and nutmeg, then bake for 6 to 8 minutes, or until the fish just flakes. Serve hot.

Sautéed or Deep-fried

Sautéed Abalone Steaks

THIS IS *the classic way to prepare this delicacy.*

S E R V E S 4

2   eggs
    Salt and pepper
¼   teaspoon garlic powder
    All-purpose flour
½   cup breadcrumbs
4   abalone steaks, pounded
3   tablespoons vegetable oil
3   tablespoons butter or margarine
    Lemon wedges

1. In a wide, shallow bowl, lightly beat the eggs and season with salt, pepper, and garlic powder.

2. Spread the flour and breadcrumbs on separate sheets of wax paper. Dredge abalone steaks in flour, dip them in the egg mixture, then press them into the breadcrumbs to coat. Place on wax paper and refrigerate for 1 hour.

3. Heat the oil and butter in a large skillet over medium-high heat, add the steaks, and sauté for 30 seconds on each side. Transfer to 4 plates with a slotted spatula and serve hot, with lemon wedges.

· · Fabulous Fish

202

Blackened Bluefish

CAJUN COOKING, with its blackened this and blackened that, is very popular these days. Imagine, all those years my mother was burning practically everything she cooked, she was actually cooking Cajun style!

S E R V E S   4

1   teaspoon sea salt
1   teaspoon whole white peppercorns
1   teaspoon whole black peppercorns
¼   teaspoon hot red pepper flakes
½   teaspoon dried thyme
4   bluefish fillets, 8 ounces each
6   tablespoons (¾ stick) butter or margarine
2   tablespoons olive oil
6   tablespoons chopped fresh coriander

1. Grind the salt, peppercorns, hot pepper flakes, and thyme in a spice mill or mash with a mortar and pestle and coat the fish thoroughly with the seasonings.

2. In a heavy cast-iron skillet, heat the butter over high heat until it is very, very hot and smoking (put on the exhaust fan to pull out the smoke).

3. Pour 1 tablespoon of the olive oil in the pan and quickly add 2 of the bluefish fillets. Cook them for 3 minutes, turning once. Transfer them to a warm plate and repeat the procedure with the other 2 fillets.

4. Before serving, brush the fillets with the melted butter in the pan and sprinkle with the coriander. Serve hot.

Bluefish with Lemon-Caper Sauce

BLUEFISH, AN *oily fish, is best when accompanied by a citrus or tomato sauce. Steamed broccoli makes a fine side dish; the bonus is that it's delicious dipped into the lemon-caper sauce.*

S E R V E S 4

4   bluefish fillets, 6 to 8 ounces each
    Salt and pepper
2   tablespoons olive oil
4   tablespoons (½ stick) butter or margarine
2   tablespoons fresh lemon juice
¼   cup drained capers

1. Season the bluefish with salt and pepper to taste.

2. In a large skillet, heat the olive oil over moderate heat until it's hot, then sauté the bluefish for 6 to 8 minutes, or until it just flakes, turning it once.

3. While the bluefish is cooking, heat the butter in a small saucepan until the foam subsides and the butter is nut brown.

4. Remove the pan from the heat and add the lemon juice and capers, swirling the pan.

5. Transfer the bluefish to 4 plates and spoon the sauce over each portion. Serve hot.

Sesame Bluefish with Gingerroot and Scallions

FOR MAXIMUM
enjoyment, serve this dish
with a heaping mound of
steaming brown rice.

S E R V E S   4

4   bluefish fillets, 6 to 8 ounces each
    all-purpose flour seasoned with salt and pepper
2   tablespoons olive oil
2   teaspoons sesame oil
One 2-inch cube peeled gingerroot, cut into
        julienne strips
4   scallions, sliced thin on the diagonal
4   lemon wedges

1. Dredge bluefish fillets in seasoned flour.

2. Heat olive oil and sesame oil in a large skillet over medium heat, then sauté the fillets for about 3 or 4 minutes on each side, until they just flake. Transfer the fillets to a platter and keep warm in a 200-degree oven.

3. In the skillet, sauté the gingerroot and scallions for about 1 minute.

4. Transfer the bluefish fillets to 4 plates and top the fillets with the gingerroot and scallion mixture. Serve hot, garnished with lemon wedges.

Deep-fried Catfish with Hush Puppies

WITH CATFISH *enjoying such tremendous popularity, here is the classic way to prepare these delectable fish. The hush puppies are a bonus.*

SERVES 4

THE HUSH PUPPIES

1 cup cornmeal
2 tablespoons baking powder
1/2 teaspoon salt
1/4 teaspoon pepper
1/3 cup minced onion
1 egg, beaten
1/4 cup milk

2 pounds catfish fillets, cut into 1/2-inch-thick
   pieces
Milk
Salt and pepper
Cayenne pepper
Cornmeal
Vegetable oil for deep-frying

1. To make the hush puppies, mix together in a bowl the cornmeal, baking powder, and salt and pepper.

2. Add minced onion and beaten egg and stir vigorously.

3. Mix in milk to make a stiff batter.

4. Form into small 2-inch patties, poke a hole through the center of each like a doughnut, and set aside.

5. Dip catfish fillets in milk that has been put in a shallow dish, then sprinkle with salt, pepper, and cayenne.

6. Dredge catfish fillets in cornmeal, covering them completely, and shake off excess.

7. In a deep skillet or wok, heat the vegetable oil over high heat until it just begins to smoke (turn on overhead fan), then deep-fry fish, turning once, until browned, about 5 minutes.

8. Remove the catfish fillets with a slotted spatula to paper towels to drain, then transfer to a platter, cover, and keep warm.

9. Fry the hush puppies in the same oil until they are crusty and brown, drain, and serve with the fish. Serve hot.

Deep-fried Catfish with Pecan Butter

THIS DISH *epitomizes Southwestern cuisine, and makes for a very showy dinner centerpiece.*

SERVES 4

THE PECAN BUTTER

⅓ cup pecan halves

2 tablespoons butter or margarine

1 tablespoon minced fresh chives, or 1 teaspoon dried

1 jalapeño chile, stemmed, seeded, and minced (wear rubber gloves)

THE BUTTER SAUCE

⅓ cup White Fish Stock (page 258)

⅓ cup dry white wine

⅓ cup white wine vinegar

1 tablespoon minced onion

2 teaspoons dried tarragon

1 cup (2 sticks) butter or margarine, cut into tablespoon-sized pieces

1 tablespoon fresh lime juice

Salt and pepper

¾ cup vegetable oil

2 eggs, beaten

½ cup buttermilk

1 cup cornmeal, preferably blue

¼ teaspoon salt

¼ teaspoon freshly ground black pepper

4 catfish fillets, 6 ounces each

1 tablespoon minced fresh chives

1. To make the pecan butter, put the pecans in a baking pan, place in a preheated 325-degree oven, and toast, stirring occasionally, until the pecans are golden, about 15 minutes. Set aside to cool.

2. In a food processor fitted with steel blade, chop the pecans, add the butter, chives, and jalapeño and blend until the mixture is puréed, about 2 minutes. Transfer to a bowl and refrigerate for at least 1 hour.

3. To make the butter sauce, bring the stock, wine, vinegar, onion, and 1 teaspoon of the tarragon to a boil in a saucepan, stirring occasionally, and boil until the mixture is reduced by half.

4. Reduce the heat to medium and whisk in the butter, one piece at a time.

5. Whisk in the remaining teaspoon tarragon and the lime juice.

6. Cut the chilled pecan butter into chunks and whisk it into the sauce as you did the regular butter, until it is thoroughly blended in. Season with salt and pepper to taste.

7. To prepare the catfish, heat the oil in a large skillet or wok until it is very hot.

8. In a bowl, whisk together the eggs and buttermilk and pour the mixture into a shallow dish.

9. In another shallow dish, mix the cornmeal with the salt and pepper.

10. Dip the catfish fillets in the egg mixture, then

dredge them in the cornmeal mixture. Coat completely and shake off any excess.

11. In the hot oil, fry the fillets until they are golden, about 3 minutes on each side. Remove from the oil with a slotted spatula and drain on paper towels.

12. Pour the sauce in the middle of 4 warm dinner plates and place a catfish fillet on top of the sauce. Garnish with chives. Serve hot.

Catfish with Potato Sticks and Artichoke Hearts

ALTHOUGH CATFISH *fillets are delicious breaded and deep-fried, or simply sautéed in butter and lemon juice, here's a recipe that brings out all the flavor of this relatively mild fish.*

S E R V E S   4

4   fresh uncooked artichoke hearts
1   lemon, cut in half
4   large catfish fillets (about 1 ½ pounds of
       catfish)
¼   teaspoon salt
¼   teaspoon freshly ground black pepper
⅛   teaspoon cayenne pepper, or to taste
1   teaspoon paprika
¼   teaspoon dried thyme
½   cup all-purpose flour
¼   cup vegetable oil
5   tablespoons butter or margarine
1   pound boiling potatoes, peeled and cut into
       1 ½-by-½-inch sticks
½   teaspoon minced garlic
¼   cup chopped fresh sage leaves
1   teaspoon fresh lemon juice

1. Slice the artichoke bottoms vertically into strips about ¼-inch thick, rub them with one half of the cut lemon, and reserve them in a bowl of water in which the juice of the other half lemon has been squeezed.

2. Cut the catfish fillets into 1 ½-by-½-inch strips.

3. In a plastic bag, combine the salt, pepper, cayenne, paprika, thyme, and flour, add the catfish strips, and shake the bag to coat the catfish with the seasoned flour.

4. In a large skillet, heat 2 tablespoons of the vegetable oil and 2 tablespoons of the butter over high heat and sauté the catfish in the mixture, stirring and tossing the strips occasionally, for 5 minutes, or until the catfish is browned. Remove the skillet from the heat and set aside.

5. In a second large skillet, heat the remaining 2 tablespoons of oil and 1 tablespoon of the remaining butter, add the potato sticks, and sauté them for 5 minutes or until they're just golden.

6. Add the sliced artichoke hearts and sauté the mixture for about 10 minutes, until the artichoke slices are tender.

7. Add the garlic, sage, the remaining 2 tablespoons of butter, and the catfish and stir the mixture gently.

8. Transfer equal portions of the mixture to each of 4 plates and drizzle each with lemon juice. Serve hot.

Crab and Shrimp with Sherry

VERMOUTH CAN *be substituted for the sherry in this delicious recipe, although I personally prefer it with the sherry.*

S E R V E S   4
T O   6

2	tablespoons butter or margarine
1½	pounds shrimp, shelled and deveined
1	pound crabmeat, picked over
	Salt and pepper
¼	cup chopped onion
½	cup dry sherry
1	cup cream or half-and-half
1	teaspoon Worcestershire sauce
12	fresh basil leaves
2	tablespoons chopped fresh parsley leaves

1. In a large frying pan, melt the butter and sauté the shrimp over high heat for 30 seconds, stirring constantly.

2. Add the crabmeat and salt and pepper to taste and cook for another minute, stirring constantly. With a slotted spoon remove the crabmeat and shrimp to a warm serving dish.

3. Add the onion and sherry to the pan liquids and cook over high heat until reduced by half.

4. Add the cream and Worcestershire sauce and reduce over high heat to 1 cup.

5. Reduce the heat to low, return the shrimp and crabmeat to the pan, stir well, and add the basil.

6. Spoon the crab, shrimp, and sherry mixture onto individual plates and garnish with the parsley leaves. Serve hot.

My Own Crab Cakes

THERE SEEM *to be as many recipes for crab cakes as there are crabs, but this version is the one I like best of the several that I have tried. (Use real crab—the ubiquitous imitation crabmeat is okay for cold salads, but doesn't work for a really top-notch crab cake.)*

S E R V E S   6

1	cup mayonnaise
2	tablespoons cracker crumbs
1/8	teaspoon cayenne pepper
1/8	teaspoon ground celery seeds
1/8	teaspoon Dijon-style mustard
1/4	teaspoon fresh lemon juice
1	egg white, lightly beaten
1	pound lump crabmeat, picked over
1 1/4	cups breadcrumbs
3	tablespoons butter or margarine
	Lemon wedges
	Tartar sauce (page 255)

1. In a large bowl, combine the mayonnaise, cracker crumbs, cayenne, celery seeds, mustard, lemon juice, and egg white and stir in the crabmeat.

2. Form the mixture into six 1/2-inch-thick cakes and coat the cakes with most of the breadcrumbs.

3. Sprinkle a large plate with the remaining breadcrumbs, transfer the crab cakes to the plate, and chill them, covered, for at least 1 hour.

4. In a large skillet, heat the butter and sauté the crab cakes, turning them once, for 4 minutes, or until they are golden.

5. Transfer the crab cakes to paper towels with a slotted spoon. Allow them to drain, then arrange them on a heated platter.

6. Garnish with lemon wedges and serve hot with tartar sauce.

Grouper-Crab Turbans with Rémoulade Sauce

ANOTHER OF *those corny, old-fashioned heavy French recipes, among the first I tried when I got into serious fish cookery. But this one reaffirms the Rapp Rule of Clichés—things only become clichés because they're worth repeating. This recipe, old hat (or old turban) though it may be, is a classic, and you should prepare it at least once.*

SERVES 4

2	pounds grouper fillets, cut into 8 thin slices about 4 inches square
	Salt and pepper
½	pound crabmeat, picked over
	Juice of 1 lime
2	tablespoons milk
1	egg
	All-purpose flour
2	tablespoons olive oil
2	tablespoons butter or margarine
	Rémoulade Sauce (page 254)

1. Season grouper slices with salt and pepper to taste, place equal amounts of crabmeat on each slice, and sprinkle with a few drops of lime juice. Roll and secure turbans with wooden toothpicks.

2. In a shallow bowl, whisk together the milk and the egg. Spread flour on a sheet of wax paper. Dip fish in egg mixture, then dredge in flour, shaking off excess.

3. Heat the oil and butter in a skillet over medium-high heat, then sauté the turbans, turning and moving them around occasionally, until they are golden and just cooked, about 6 to 8 minutes.

4. With a slotted spoon, remove the turbans and place 2 each on 4 heated dinner plates. Spoon on rémoulade sauce and serve hot.

Halibut with Avocado-Cream Sauce

I LOVE avocados. If only they weren't so bloody fattening! But what the heck, we've got to throw caution to the winds once in a while. So I always taste my sauce and add more avocado at least two or three times before I'm satisfied. If you're like me, better buy at least one extra avocado when you shop for this recipe.

SERVES 4

½ cup dry white wine
1 tablespoon minced shallot
2 ripe Haas avocados
1 tablespoon fresh lemon juice
½ cup cream or half-and-half
⅛ teaspoon cayenne pepper
2 tablespoons vegetable oil or olive oil
2 pounds halibut fillets, cut into ½-inch-thick
   slices
   Salt and pepper
   Lemon slices

1. In a small saucepan, combine the wine, shallot, and ⅓ cup water, bring the liquid to a boil, then reduce the heat and simmer the mixture for 5 minutes.

2. Halve the avocados lengthwise, remove the pits, and peel each half. Slice half of 1 avocado lengthwise into thin slices, sprinkle with 1 teaspoon lemon juice to prevent discoloration, and reserve for garnish. Purée the remaining 3 avocado halves in a blender or food processor fitted with the steel blade.

3. With the motor of the blender or food processor still running, strain the wine mixture through a sieve into the purée, spin for a couple of seconds, then transfer the purée to a small saucepan.

4. Whisk in the cream, the remaining 2 teaspoons

lemon juice, and cayenne, and place over low heat until sauce is just heated through. Cover and keep warm.

5. In a skillet, heat the vegetable or olive oil and sauté the halibut slices for 2 to 3 minutes, or until they just flake, turning them once. Season with salt and pepper to taste.

6. Divide the sauce among 4 heated plates, then arrange the halibut slices on the sauce. Garnish with the reserved sliced avocado and the lemon slices and serve hot.

Mahimahi with Mangoes in Green Peppercorn Sauce

THERE'S PRACTICALLY *no taste in the world as good as warm mango.*

S E R V E S 4

4 mahimahi fillets, 6 to 8 ounces each
1 tablespoon fresh lime juice
3 tablespoons all-purpose flour
Salt and pepper
¼ cup olive oil
3 tablespoons butter or margarine
2 large, ripe mangoes, peeled and sliced
2 tablespoons green peppercorns in water, drained
½ cup cream or half-and-half
Watercress sprigs

1. Place mahimahi fillets in a shallow glass dish and sprinkle with lime juice. Chill, covered with foil, for 1 hour.

2. Combine flour with salt and pepper and dredge fish in the mixture, shaking off the excess.

3. In a large skillet, heat the olive oil over medium-high heat, and sauté the mahimahi fillets for 3 or 4 minutes on each side, until the fish just flakes. Transfer to a platter and keep warm, covered.

4. In a clean skillet, melt 2 tablespoons of the butter and sauté the mango slices for 2 minutes. Arrange them around the fish.

5. Melt the remaining tablespoon of butter in the skillet, add the green peppercorns, and sauté 1 minute.

6. Add the cream and boil for 3 minutes, or until it is reduced by half.

7. Spoon sauce over fish and serve hot, garnished with sprigs of watercress.

Mahimahi with Sun-dried Tomatoes and Basil Sauce

I REALLY like sun-dried tomatoes. I buy them dry in the bag, like prunes, because they're much cheaper that way. Then I soak them in olive oil and garlic until they soften up. I always keep a jar on hand in the fridge just in case. A spinach pasta with just a bit of butter or margarine is a great side dish with this recipe.

S E R V E S   6

1 ½   cups dry white wine
½   cup white wine vinegar
4   shallots, peeled and minced
¾   cup cream or half-and-half
1   cup (2 sticks) butter or margarine, cut up
½   cup chopped, softened sun-dried tomatoes (you may use bottled, softened sun-dried tomatoes or soften the packaged variety by soaking in warm water for about half an hour)
¼   cup chopped fresh basil leaves, plus whole basil leaves for garnish
6   mahimahi fillets, 6 to 8 ounces each
    Salt and pepper
4   tablespoons olive oil

1. In a saucepan, combine the wine, vinegar, and shallots and boil the mixture until the liquid is reduced by half.

2. Add the cream and boil the mixture until the liquid is again reduced by half.

3. Reduce the heat to low and whisk in the butter or margarine, one piece at a time.

4. Stir in the sun-dried tomatoes and the chopped basil, cover the pan, and remove it from the heat.

5. Season the mahimahi fillets with salt and pepper to taste.

6. In a large skillet, heat the olive oil. Sauté the

mahimahi fillets for 6 to 8 minutes, turning once, until they just flake.

7. Transfer the fillets to six heated plates, spoon the sauce over each fillet, and garnish with basil leaves. Serve hot.

Monkfish Medallions with Tomato-Lemon Sauce

I REMEMBER *cadging this recipe from the chef of an excellent little mama-papa restaurant in Greenwich Village. The food was sensational, but there's no business more cruel than the restaurant business and alas, the delightful Belgian couple's establishment went out of business three years ago. Luckily, this recipe lives on to remind me of their quaint, homey cafe.*

S E R V E S   4

4 monkfish fillets (about 2 pounds), cut crosswise into 1-inch-thick medallions
1 ½ teaspoons dried thyme, crumbled
Salt and pepper
4 tablespoons (½ stick) butter or margarine
4 garlic cloves, peeled and minced
2 cups coarsely chopped fresh tomatoes
2 tablespoons fresh lemon juice
2 tablespoons minced fresh parsley leaves

1. Season the monkfish fillets with 1 teaspoon of the dried thyme and salt and pepper.

2. In a large skillet, melt 2 tablespoons of the butter over high heat and in it sauté the monkfish, turning it once, for 8 minutes, or until it is cooked through.

3. Divide the monkfish fillets among 4 heated plates and keep them warm, covered.

4. In the skillet, sauté the garlic in the remaining 2 tablespoons butter over moderately low heat, stirring, until it is golden.

5. Add the tomatoes, lemon juice, and the remaining ½ teaspoon thyme and cook the sauce, stirring, for 5 minutes.

6. Stir in any juices that have accumulated on the plates, along with the parsley and salt and pepper to taste, and spoon the sauce over the monkfish. Serve hot.

Red Snapper Moroccan Style

ALTHOUGH I *usually use red snapper fillets for this recipe, you may substitute sea bass, halibut, or cod.*

S E R V E S 4

THE MARINADE

8   cloves garlic, peeled and chopped
1   teaspoon salt
2   teaspoons paprika
2   teaspoons ground cumin
⅛   teaspoon cayenne pepper (or less to taste)
½   cup chopped fresh cilantro leaves
    Juice of 1 lemon

2   pounds red snapper fillets, cut into 2-inch
        pieces
⅓   cup all-purpose flour
2   tablespoons olive oil
4   sprigs cilantro

1. To make the marinade, blend the garlic with the salt, paprika, cumin, and cayenne in a blender or food processor fitted with the steel blade until the mixture takes on a pasty consistency.

2. Transfer the garlic paste to a small bowl, add the cilantro and lemon juice, and stir until the mixture is well blended.

3. Cover the snapper pieces with the marinade and let stand for 1 hour, covered.

4. Dredge the red snapper pieces in the flour and shake off the excess.

5. In a large skillet, heat the olive oil over medium-high heat and sauté the red snapper for 3 minutes on each side, or until it is just golden and cooked through.

6. Remove to a platter and garnish with cilantro sprigs. Serve hot.

Red Snapper with Tomato Sauce and Bananas

I FIRST did this recipe on a dare. A friend of mine didn't think I had the stamina, the patience, or the powers of concentration. It wasn't easy the first time, but once I tasted the heavenly results it got easier.

SERVES 4

THE TOMATO SAUCE

2 tablespoons olive oil
1/2 cup chopped onion
2 garlic cloves, peeled and minced
2 cups peeled, seeded, and chopped fresh or canned tomatoes
1/4 teaspoon sugar
1/4 teaspoon dried oregano
1/4 teaspoon dried basil
Salt and pepper

10 tablespoons (1 1/4 sticks) butter or margarine
4 bananas, peeled and halved lengthwise, then halved crosswise
1 teaspoon Worcestershire sauce
1/4 cup fresh lemon juice
1 teaspoon salt
1/4 teaspoon white pepper
2 eggs
2 tablespoons milk
1/2 cup plus 1 tablespoon vegetable oil
4 red snapper fillets, 6 to 8 ounces each
1 cup all-purpose flour
1 tablespoon chopped fresh parsley leaves

1. To make the tomato sauce, heat the olive oil in a saucepan over moderate heat, add the onion and garlic, and sauté, stirring, until the onion is soft.

2. Add the tomatoes, sugar, oregano, and basil and simmer the sauce, stirring occasionally, for about 10 minutes. Add salt and pepper to taste. Set aside and keep warm.

3. In a skillet, melt 2 tablespoons of butter over moderately high heat and sauté the bananas for about 2 minutes on each side, until they are slightly browned. Transfer them to a platter and keep them warm in a 200-degree oven.

4. In a small bowl, combine the Worcestershire sauce, 2 tablespoons of the lemon juice, and the salt and white pepper. Stir.

5. In a shallow dish, whisk together the eggs, milk, and 1 tablespoon vegetable oil.

6. Rub the Worcestershire mixture into the fillets and dredge them in the flour.

7. In a large skillet, heat the remaining ½ cup vegetable oil until it is hot but not smoking.

8. While the oil is heating, dip the fillets in the egg mixture, making sure that each is completely coated in egg.

9. Sauté the fillets in the vegetable oil for 3 minutes over medium heat, then turn them and sauté for 2 or 3 minutes more, until they just flake.

10. Transfer the fillets to the platter containing the bananas, spoon the tomato sauce over them, and return them to the 200-degree oven to keep warm.

11. Pour the oil out of the skillet. Add the remaining 8 tablespoons butter and melt over high heat.

12. Add the remaining 2 tablespoons lemon juice and the parsley to the melted butter.

13. Remove the platter containing the snapper fillets, bananas, and tomato sauce from the oven and spoon the butter mixture over all. Serve hot.

Salmon in Vodka-Cream Sauce with Green Peppercorns

NO OFFENSE *meant, but some recipes have a very yuppie sound. Or perhaps trendy would be a more appropriate adjective. This is one of those—and it's every bit as good as all the others!*

S E R V E S   6

6	salmon fillets, 6 to 8 ounces each
	Salt and pepper
3	tablespoons olive oil
1½	cups cream or half-and-half
½	cup vodka
2	tablespoons green peppercorns in water, drained and crushed
4	tablespoons (½ stick) butter or margarine
3	tablespoons fresh lime juice
	Cooked spinach
¼	cup snipped fresh chives

1. Season salmon with salt and pepper to taste.

2. In a large skillet, heat the oil over medium-high heat, add salmon, and sauté about 6 to 8 minutes, turning once. Using a slotted spatula, transfer the salmon fillets to a serving platter and cover to keep warm.

3. Pour excess oil from skillet, then add the cream and vodka and boil until the mixture is slightly thickened, about 4 minutes.

4. Add green peppercorns and butter and stir until butter is just melted.

5. Mix in lime juice and season with salt and pepper to taste.

6. Spoon cooked spinach onto 6 warm plates and top each with a salmon fillet. Spoon the sauce over and sprinkle with fresh chives. Serve hot.

Bay Scallops in Garlic-Butter Sauce

THIS IS a classic, easy way to prepare this succulent little shellfish. Serve with a mélange of sautéed, julienned red, green, and yellow peppers.

S E R V E S   4

¼ teaspoon freshly grated lemon zest
¼ cup minced fresh parsley leaves
4 tablespoons (½ stick) butter or margarine
2 garlic cloves, peeled and minced
1½ pounds bay scallops
½ cup dry white wine
Salt and pepper

1. In a bowl, toss together the lemon zest and parsley and reserve the mixture.

2. In a heavy skillet, melt the butter over medium-high heat and sauté the garlic, stirring, until it is golden.

3. Add the scallops and cook them, stirring occasionally, for 2 minutes, or until they are just firm, and transfer them with a slotted spoon to a platter.

4. Add the wine to the pan juices, boil the mixture, stirring, until it is reduced to about ½ cup, and season with salt and pepper to taste.

5. Spoon the sauce over the scallops, then sprinkle with the reserved parsley mixture. Serve hot.

Bay Scallops with Mustard-Thyme Mayonnaise

I AM a big mustard fan. I'll bet I have at least ten different kinds of mustard in my pantry. (I win. I just checked and there are 13.) Last night, in fact, I broiled a thick, juicy halibut fillet coated with a hot Louisiana mustard and garlic and it was just sensational. So is this dish.

SERVES 4

1   cup mayonnaise
2   teaspoons chopped fresh thyme or ½ teaspoon
       dried thyme, crumbled
2   tablespoons coarse-grained Dijon-style mustard
1   teaspoon fresh lemon juice
1½   pounds bay scallops
       All-purpose flour
2   tablespoons butter or margarine
2   tablespoons olive oil

1. Whisk together the mayonnaise, thyme, mustard, and lemon juice in a small bowl and chill the sauce, covered, for 1 hour.

2. In a large shallow dish, dredge the scallops in the flour, shaking off the excess.

3. In a large skillet, heat the butter and oil over medium-high heat and sauté the scallops, shaking the skillet, for 3 to 4 minutes, or until they are golden.

4. Serve the scallops hot with the chilled sauce.

Shrimp with Lime and Avocado

ANOTHER RECIPE *worth the cholesterol, at least once in your life.*

SERVES 6

2   pounds shrimp, shelled and deveined
¼   cup fresh lime juice
    Salt and white pepper
2   ripe avocados
2   tablespoons butter or margarine
2   tablespoons finely chopped shallots
⅓   cup tequila
1   cup cream or half-and-half
¼   teaspoon hot red pepper flakes, or to taste
¼   cup chopped fresh coriander leaves
    Cooked rice

1. In a mixing bowl, combine the shrimp, 3 tablespoons of the lime juice, and salt and pepper to taste. Let the shrimp marinate for 1 hour.

2. Peel and pit the avocados, and cut into ½-inch slices. Place the slices in a bowl, add the remaining tablespoon of lime juice so the avocado flesh does not discolor, and mix gently.

3. In a large frying pan, melt the butter, then add the shrimp and its marinade and cook over high heat, stirring constantly, for 1 minute.

4. Sprinkle the shallots over the shrimp and cook, stirring, for about 15 seconds, then add the tequila, cream, and hot pepper flakes. Mix gently, then add the avocado slices and cook for 1 more minute.

5. With a slotted spoon, transfer the shrimp and avocado slices to warm plates.

6. Bring the sauce to a full boil for about 1 minute, then add the coriander. Remove the sauce from the heat and spoon it over the shrimp and avocado. Serve hot with rice.

Shrimp with Mushroom-Watercress Sauce

SCALLOPS MAY be substituted for the shrimp in this recipe, which features one of the most flavorful sauces in my entire repertoire. Hot, fat, home-fried potatoes go wonderfully well with this dish.

S E R V E S 6

2 pounds shrimp, shelled and deveined
1 bunch watercress, large stems removed
2 tablespoons butter or margarine
½ pound mushrooms, quartered
3 tablespoons finely chopped onion
2 cloves garlic, peeled and minced
¾ cup dry white wine
   Salt and pepper
⅛ teaspoon hot red pepper flakes
1 cup cream or half-and-half
2 tablespoons Pernod or anisette

1. Halve each shrimp crosswise and set aside.

2. In a large saucepan, boil enough water to cover the watercress, add the watercress and blanch for 2 minutes, or until it wilts. Drain well and rinse under cold water, squeeze to extract the liquid, then chop coarsely.

3. Melt the butter in a saucepan over medium-high heat, add the mushrooms, and sauté, stirring constantly, for 1 minute. Stir in the onion and garlic and sauté for 1 more minute. Add the wine and cook briskly for 5 minutes, until the wine has almost evaporated.

4. Add the shrimp and sprinkle with salt, pepper, and hot pepper flakes. Cook for 2 minutes, stirring frequently. Remove the shrimp from the pan with a slotted spoon and set aside.

5. Add ¾ cup of the cream to the contents of the saucepan and cook for 1 minute over high heat.

6. Stir in the watercress and cook for 1 more minute.

7. Empty the saucepan into a blender or food processor fitted with the steel blade and purée until smooth.

8. Put the shrimp into a saucepan. Add the mushroom-watercress sauce and the remaining ¼ cup cream and simmer until the shrimp is just warm. Stir in the Pernod and serve hot.

Classic Sole Meunière

HERE IS *the most basic yet classic method of preparing any type of sole. Quick and easy, it brings out all the delicate taste of this elegant fish.*

S E R V E S 4

4 sole fillets, 6 to 8 ounces each
1 cup milk
   All-purpose flour
6 tablespoons (¾ stick) butter or margarine
2 tablespoons olive oil
2 tablespoons fresh lemon juice
1 tablespoon minced fresh parsley leaves

1. Dip the sole in the milk, then dredge with the flour, shaking off the excess.

2. In a skillet, heat 2 tablespoons of the butter and the olive oil over medium-high heat. Sauté the fish until it's brown and crispy on both sides, about 3 minutes on each side.

3. Make sauce by heating the remaining 4 tablespoons of butter in a saucepan until it's bubbly, add the lemon juice and parsley, and pour over the fish. Serve hot.

Lemon Sole with Ginger Meunière

GRAY SOLE, flounder, or halibut may be substituted in this quick and easy recipe, which is just a slight—but interesting—variation on Classic Sole Meunière.

S E R V E S   4

Salt and pepper

½ cup all-purpose flour

4 lemon sole fillets, about 8 ounces each, or 8 smaller fillets (total weight about 2 pounds)

8 tablespoons (1 stick) butter or margarine

1 tablespoon freshly grated gingerroot

4 scallions, chopped

3 tablespoons lemon juice

1. Mix the salt and pepper with the flour in a shallow pan or dish.

2. Dredge the fillets in the seasoned flour, coating both sides, and shake off the excess.

3. In a large skillet, melt the butter over medium-high heat and sauté the fillets for 2 minutes on each side. Remove with a slotted spatula to a warm serving platter.

4. Add the ginger, scallions and lemon juice to the butter remaining in the skillet, cook, stirring, for 30 seconds, then pour over the fish. Serve hot.

Sole Piccata with Sherry and Capers

THIS IS *the best way to prepare sole I've ever come across. The combination of the sour lemons, the sweet sherry, the salty capers, and the delicate sole is absolutely super. If you make it during the spring or early summer, serve it with steamed asparagus.*

S E R V E S   4

2 eggs
½ cup milk
1 teaspoon salt
Freshly ground pepper
½ teaspoon paprika
2 pounds sole fillets
1 cup all-purpose flour
3 tablespoons butter or margarine
3 tablespoons olive oil
¾ cup dry sherry
½ cup lemon juice
8 lemon slices
¼ cup drained capers
¼ cup minced fresh parsley leaves

1. In a shallow bowl, beat the eggs lightly, add the milk, salt, pepper to taste, and paprika and blend well.

2. Dip the fillets in the egg mixture, then dredge them in the flour, shaking off the excess.

3. In a large skillet, heat 2 tablespoons of the butter and 2 tablespoons of the olive oil over medium heat and sauté the fillets in batches for 2 minutes on each side, or until they just flake.

4. With a slotted spatula transfer the fillets to a platter and keep them warm.

5. Add the remaining tablespoon of butter and the remaining tablespoon of olive oil to the skillet, add the sherry, and boil the mixture over high heat for 1 minute.

6. Add the lemon juice and bring the mixture to a boil again.

7. Return the sole fillets to the skillet, add the lemon slices, and heat the mixture for 30 seconds.

8. Transfer the fillets to a platter, top them with the sauce, and sprinkle them with capers and parsley. Serve hot.

Sautéed Swordfish in Soy Marinade

THIS DELICIOUS
marinade can be used with shark, halibut, tuna, and salmon as well, and you can broil or grill the steaks instead of sautéeing them.

S E R V E S   4

4 swordfish steaks, about 1 inch thick and 6 to 8 ounces each
2 tablespoons soy sauce
¼ cup fresh lemon juice
   Salt and freshly ground pepper
½ cup plus 2 tablespoons olive oil
8 lemon slices, halved
   Fresh parsley leaves and sprigs

1. Arrange the swordfish in a nonreactive baking pan or glass dish.

2. In a small bowl, whisk together the soy sauce, lemon juice, and salt and pepper to taste, add ½ cup of the olive oil, whisking, and whisk the marinade until it is emulsified.

3. Pour the marinade over the swordfish steaks, turn the steaks to coat them, and let them marinate, covered, turning them occasionally, for 1 hour in the refrigerator.

4. In a large heavy skillet, heat the remaining 2 tablespoons olive oil until it is hot but not smoking, add the swordfish steaks, and sauté for 8 to 10 minutes, turning once, until they are browned on each side and just cooked through.

5. Transfer to warm plates and garnish with lemon slices and parsley. Serve hot.

Sesame Tilefish Slices

MY YOUNGER daughter, Danielle, fell in love with sesame a couple of years ago. Everything she ate had to have sesame oil or sesame seeds on it. So one night when she came over for dinner, I went to my pantry, said "Open sesame," and the following recipe resulted. I'm almost embarrassed to say I served it to her with sesame noodles.

S E R V E S   4

2 pounds tilefish fillets
¼ cup sesame seeds
¼ cup soy sauce
½ teaspoon sesame oil
3 tablespoons vegetable oil
½ cup minced scallions
¼ teaspoon pepper

1. Cut the tilefish fillets into ½-inch slices and set aside.

2. In a heavy skillet, heat the sesame seeds over medium-high heat until they begin to turn golden.

3. Purée the sesame seeds in a blender with the soy sauce, sesame oil, and 1 tablespoon of the vegetable oil. Put this mixture into a shallow bowl, add the scallions and pepper, and blend well.

4. Heat the remaining 2 tablespoons oil in a large skillet or wok. Dip the fish slices into the sesame seed mixture and sauté them until they are golden brown on both sides. Serve hot.

Trout Amandine

THIS IS *truly a classic dish and very easy to prepare. Not only is this great for dinner, it also makes a wonderful lunch—or even breakfast—dish!*

S E R V E S   4

1   egg
1   cup milk
8   trout fillets, 4 ounces each
    All-purpose flour
½   cup (1 stick) butter or margarine
½   cup slivered almonds
2   tablespoons fresh lemon juice
2   tablespoons Worcestershire sauce
1   tablespoon minced fresh parsley leaves

1. In a shallow dish, whisk the egg and milk together, dip in the trout fillets until they're covered, then dredge them in the flour, shaking off the excess.

2. In a large skillet, heat the butter over medium-high heat and sauté the fillets for 3 to 4 minutes on each side, until they just flake. Transfer the trout fillets to a platter and keep warm in a 200-degree oven.

3. Add the almonds to the skillet and stir them over moderate heat for about 1 minute.

4. Add the lemon juice, Worcestershire sauce, and parsley, and cook the mixture, stirring, until it is heated through.

5. Transfer 2 trout fillets to each of 4 warm plates, and spoon the sauce over the trout. Serve hot.

Sauces and Stocks

Basic White Sauce and Sauce Mornay

THESE CLASSIC *sauces go well with any fish, any time.*

**M A K E S
2 C U P S**

3 tablespoons butter or margarine
3 tablespoons all-purpose flour
2 cups milk
   Salt
   White pepper

1. In a saucepan, melt the butter. Add the flour and whisk constantly for 3 to 4 minutes.

2. When the mixture is smooth, remove from the heat and add the milk, whisking until the mixture is lump-free.

3. Return to stove and cook over medium heat, stirring constantly, until the sauce is creamy and thick. Season to taste with salt and white pepper.

Sauce Mornay

To 2 cups of basic white sauce add ¼ cup grated Swiss cheese and ¼ cup grated Parmesan cheese. Stir over low heat until the cheeses melt.

Beurre Blanc

THE CLASSIC French sauce for fish. Once you've made your basic beurre blanc, you can add any other flavors you want.

MAKES
ABOUT
½ CUP

2 tablespoons minced shallots
2 tablespoons white wine vinegar
2 tablespoons dry white wine
8 tablespoons (1 stick) butter or margarine, cut into pieces
Salt and pepper

1. In a small saucepan, cook the shallots in the vinegar and wine over medium-high heat, until the liquid is reduced to about 3 tablespoons.

2. Add 1 tablespoon cold water, reduce heat to low, and whisk in the butter, one piece at a time, until the butter is melted.

3. Remove the pan from the heat and whisk in salt and pepper to taste.

Herbed Butter Sauce

THIS DELICIOUS sauce *can be served over practically any fish, but it's particularly good with the codfish loaf on page 175.*

M A K E S
A B O U T
1½ C U P S

1 cup White Fish Stock (page 258) or bottled clam juice
⅓ cup minced scallions
¼ cup dry white wine
¼ cup cream or half-and-half
1 tomato, peeled, seeded, and chopped
2 tablespoons chopped fresh dill
2 tablespoons finely chopped fresh parsley leaves
7 tablespoons (⅞ stick) butter or margarine
1 tablespoon all-purpose flour
2 tablespoons fresh lemon juice
Salt and pepper

1. In a saucepan, combine fish stock, scallions, wine, and cream. Over high heat, boil until the mixture is reduced to 1 cup.

2. Add tomato, dill, and parsley, whisking to blend.

3. Knead together 1 tablespoon of the butter, softened, and the flour until it is blended. Add to the liquid, whisking until the liquid is thickened.

4. Remove the pan from the heat and whisk in the remaining 6 tablespoons of butter, 1 tablespoon at a time, until the mixture is well blended.

5. Add lemon juice and season with salt and pepper to taste. Serve hot.

Sun-dried Tomato Butter

SUN-DRIED TOMATOES *have a piquant, tangy taste and are very good combined with practically anything. This should be cut into chunks and put onto your hot fish fillets just before serving. It's also great on hot corn bread.*

MAKES ¾ CUP

½ cup (1 stick) butter or margarine, softened
⅓ cup chopped sun-dried tomatoes (if stored in oil, drain them; if dried, soften them for 30 minutes in hot water)
½ teaspoon dried basil
Salt and pepper

In a bowl cream the butter with the sun-dried tomatoes, basil, and salt and pepper to taste, until the mixture is well blended. Roll into a log shape, wrap in plastic wrap, and chill. (This mixture can also be frozen for future use.)

Tarragon Sauce

THIS SAUCE is great with any firm-fleshed white fish such as halibut, sea bass, flounder, sole, or scrod. It can be frozen.

**M A K E S
A B O U T
2½ C U P S**

6 tablespoons (¾ stick) butter or margarine
2 shallots, peeled and minced
1 tablespoon dried tarragon
¼ cup all-purpose flour
4 cups White Fish Stock (page 258) reduced to 1 cup
2½ cups cream or half-and-half
2 tablespoons dry white wine
Salt and cayenne pepper

1. In a saucepan, melt the butter over medium heat. Add the shallots and tarragon and sauté until the shallots are soft, about 3 minutes.

2. Stir in flour and cook 2 minutes over low heat.

3. Gradually add fish stock and cream, whisking, and cook until the sauce thickens.

4. Add wine, stir, and season with salt and cayenne to taste. Serve hot, poured on fish.

Aioli

THIS IS a classic garlic-flavored sauce that goes wonderfully well with almost any fish, especially red snapper, whitefish, blackfish, tilefish, or orange roughy.

MAKES ABOUT 1 CUP

1 tablespoon minced garlic
1 egg yolk
1 tablespoon Dijon-style mustard
  Salt and pepper
1 cup olive oil

1. In a mortar, crush the garlic with a pestle.

2. Put the garlic, egg yolk, mustard, and salt and pepper to taste in a mixing bowl. Add the oil gradually while beating with a whisk. Keep whisking until all the oil is incorporated and the aioli is smooth and thick. Serve hot or at room temperature.

Pesto Sauce

MOST OFTEN *used as a sauce for pasta, pesto adds a true gourmet touch to many fish, especially shark, swordfish, and halibut.*

MAKES ABOUT 2½ CUPS

2   cups fresh basil leaves
¼   cup parsley sprigs
2   cloves garlic, peeled
3   peeled walnut halves
¼   cup pine nuts
½   cup Parmesan cheese
½   cup olive oil

Combine everything in a blender or food processor fitted with the steel blade and finely chop until all the ingredients are well blended. Serve at room temperature.

Another Tomato Sauce

JUST WHAT it says—but it's not just another tomato sauce, it's an extraordinary one. Enjoy on white, flaky fish.

MAKES
ABOUT
3 CUPS

6 large ripe tomatoes, peeled and seeded
1 tablespoon olive oil
1 teaspoon finely chopped garlic
2 tablespoons diced, roasted peeled red bell pepper
⅛ teaspoon dried basil
⅛ teaspoon dried tarragon
⅛ teaspoon dried chervil
4 Greek olives, minced
Salt and pepper

1. In a blender or food processor fitted with the steel blade, purée 5 tomatoes until smooth. Push through strainer into a saucepan.

2. To the saucepan add the olive oil, garlic, red pepper, basil, tarragon, chervil, and olives. Season with salt and pepper to taste.

3. Simmer over medium-low heat until sauce is reduced by half. Dice and add remaining tomato. Heat through. Serve hot.

Tomato-Horseradish Sauce

*A **ZINGY** sauce that goes well with almost any white-fleshed fish, especially flounder.*

M A K E S
A B O U T
2¼ C U P S

1 tablespoon olive oil
2 cups peeled, seeded, and diced fresh tomatoes
3 cloves garlic, peeled and minced
2 teaspoons dried oregano leaves, crushed
1 bay leaf
1 cup tomato juice
1 tablespoon balsamic vinegar
¼ teaspoon freshly ground black pepper
2 tablespoons prepared horseradish
2 tablespoons butter or margarine, cut up

1. In a large skillet, heat the oil over medium heat, add the tomatoes, garlic, oregano, and bay leaf, and cook for 10 minutes, stirring occasionally.

2. Add the tomato juice, vinegar, and pepper and simmer for 20 minutes, stirring occasionally, until the sauce is thickened.

3. Discard the bay leaf. Stir in the horseradish and butter and heat until the butter melts. Serve hot.

Rémoulade
Sauce

YOU WHIP *this delicious sauce up in minutes and spread it on just about any fish you're about to bake or broil except bluefish, which prefers an acid-based sauce.*

M A K E S
A B O U T
1½ C U P S

1   cup mayonnaise
½   teaspoon Dijon-style mustard
1   teaspoon fresh lemon juice
½   teaspoon anchovy paste
1   teaspoon grated onion
¼   teaspoon dried tarragon
2   tablespoons drained capers

In a bowl, combine all the ingredients and stir until they are blended well. Refrigerate for storage, but heat to serve.

Tartar Sauce

THIS IS *a traditional accompaniment to deep-fried or broiled fish. I used to make tartar sauce by simply mixing mayonnaise with pickle relish. This recipe is a bit more elaborate, but worth the extra few minutes' effort.*

**M A K E S
A B O U T
1½ C U P S**

1 egg yolk
1 tablespoon white wine vinegar
2 tablespoons Dijon-style mustard
   Salt and pepper
1 cup vegetable oil
2 tablespoons fresh lemon juice
¼ cup minced onion
2 tablespoons chopped drained capers
¼ cup chopped sour pickles
¼ cup chopped fresh parsley leaves

1. Put the egg yolk, vinegar, mustard, and salt and pepper to taste in a mixing bowl and whisk for 15 seconds.

2. Add the oil gradually, beating with the whisk until all the oil has been incorporated and the sauce emulsifies.

3. Add the lemon juice, minced onion, chopped capers, sour pickles, and parsley and blend well. Cover and chill. Serve cold or at room temperature.

Sesame-Orange Sauce

I GOT this recipe from a Japanese friend of mine who, when he wasn't working nights as a sushi chef, was cooking lunch in an upscale Chinese restaurant! This sauce is delicious on any kind of fish.

MAKES ABOUT 1 CUP

3	tablespoons soy sauce
1	tablespoon sesame oil
1	teaspoon grated fresh gingerroot
3	tablespoons rice vinegar
½	cup orange juice
1	teaspoon grated orange rind

In a bowl combine all the ingredients and whisk until well blended.

Court Bouillon

COURT BOUILLON *is
ideal for poaching almost
any kind of fish, and will
keep for up to a month in
the refrigerator.*

**M A K E S
A B O U T
2 Q U A R T S**

3 cups dry white wine
2 tablespoons white wine vinegar
2 onions, peeled and cut into thick slices
   Several sprigs parsley
4 whole peppercorns
2 bay leaves
1 whole clove

1. In a large saucepan, combine all the ingredients with 4 cups cold water. Bring to a boil, then reduce heat and simmer for 30 minutes.

2. Strain the court bouillon and discard the solids.

Sauces and Stocks

257

White Fish Stock

RECIPES THAT call for fish stock or water are always better when you use fish stock. Not a million times better, but definitely better. Make lots of fish stock and keep it refrigerated or frozen for times when the need arises. It will keep for a couple of weeks refrigerated and months in a jar in the freezer.

MAKES
ABOUT
3 CUPS

2 tablespoons butter or margarine
1 pound bones and trimmings of sole, flounder, or whiting, chopped
1 cup sliced onion
12 parsley stems
2 tablespoons fresh lemon juice
½ teaspoon salt
½ cup dry white wine

1. In a large saucepan, melt the butter over medium-high heat and add the fish bones and trimmings, onion, parsley, lemon juice, salt, and ½ cup water and cook the mixture, covered, over medium heat for 5 minutes, stirring occasionally.

2. Add 3 more cups of water and the wine, bring the liquid to a boil, skimming the froth with a slotted spoon, and cook over medium heat for 30 minutes.

3. Strain the stock through a sieve into a bowl or glass jar and let it cool. The stock may be frozen for later use.

Beer Batter

YOU CAN *deep-fry almost any kind of fish in this beer batter, including squid, shrimp, and scallops.*

**M A K E S
3 C U P S**

1   cup all-purpose flour
    Salt and pepper
2   eggs, separated
2   cups beer, at room temperature
2   tablespoons vegetable oil

1. Put the flour, salt and pepper to taste, and the egg yolks in a mixing bowl and beat with a whisk. Stir in the beer and oil, cover, and set aside.

2. In another mixing bowl, beat the egg whites until they form soft peaks and fold them into the batter. Refrigerate the mixture until ready to use.

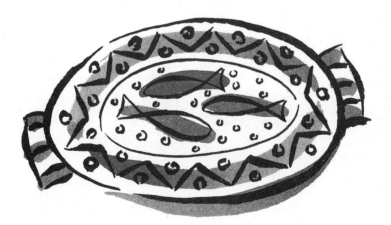

Epilogue

Well, we've come to the end of another one. And frankly, I'm elated. I quite honestly feel I have done what I set out to do—put together an outstanding selection of fish recipes that I hope will get you started on an exciting adventure in fish cookery. Don't forget that ultimately you are the artist, the skillet is your palette, the kitchen is your studio, and these recipes are just sketches for you to expand on.

Until we meet again, most appropriately . . .

Index

Abalone:
about, 18
steaks; sautéed, 202
Aioli, 250
Anchovies:
in escabeche, 41–42
Anisette and fennel, halibut fillets with,
180
Appetizers, 41–55
clams in cream sauce, 52–53
clams on the half shell with
shallot-wine sauce, 48
escabeche, 41–42
lobster medallions with avocado,
mango, and basil sauce, 43–44
oysters with orange butter, warm, 54
sea bass seviche, 49
seafood sausage, 45–46
smoked trout and horseradish with
avocado, 47
trout with apple cream sauce, 55
tuna caper dip with crudités, 50
tuna tartare, 51
Apple cream sauce, trout with, 55

Baking techniques, 13
Bananas, red snapper with tomato sauce
and, 226–28
Barbecuing techniques: See Grilling
techniques
Bass:
about, 18–19
sea
with anisette and fennel (substitute),
180
baked, with brandy and orange
sauce, 190
baked, with carrot and fennel
(substitute), 199–200
baked, with goat cheese and
Pernod, 191–92
with caper-cream sauce, 154
with curry and green chile sauce
(variation), 111
Moroccan style (substitute), 224
in parchment packets, 193
provençale, 157–58

with puréed vegetables and caviar,
155–56
salad with carrots and tomatoes;
cooked, 76
seviche, 49
and tarragon sauce for, 249
striped
baked, with caviar butter, 197
and shrimp casserole, 198
Beurre blanc, 246
Blackened bluefish, 203
Blackfish:
and aioli for, 250
Bluefish:
about, 19
fillets
baked, with farmer cheese, yogurt,
and mint, 170
baked, with sour cream and tomato
sauce, 173
blackened, 203
with gingerroot and scallions;
sesame, 205
with lemon-caper sauce, 204
with lemon-caper sauce, 204
whole
baked, with raisins and rice, 171–72
Broiling techniques, 12–13
Butters: See Sauces

Canadian Rule, 11, 37
Catfish:
about, 19–20
baked, with filberts and cheddar
(variation), 201
deep-fried, with hush puppies,
206–207
deep-fried, with pecan butter, 208–10
potato salad, 75
with potato sticks and artichoke
hearts, 211–12
with sesame seeds, 174
Caviar:
butter; baked striped bass fillets with,
197
sea bass with puréed vegetables and,
155–56
shrimp with cabbage and, 161–62

Celery shrimp chowder, 69
Chowders: See Soups
Clam(s):
about, 20
chowder; my favorite, 65–66
in cream sauce, 52–53
and fennel soup, 56–57
on the half shell with shallot-wine
sauce, 48
sauce; pasta with white, 87–88
scrod in parsley sauce with, 150
in seafood risotto, 97–98
Cod:
about, 20–21
with broccoli-cream sauce (substitute),
148–49
broiled, with shrimp-butter sauce
(substitute), 112
with curry and green chile sauce
(variation), 111
loaf with herbed butter sauce,
175–76
Moroccan style (substitute), 224–25
salad with carrots and tomatoes;
cooked, 76
steaks with green peppers (substitute),
80
in tomato-mushroom sauce
(substitute), 131–32
see also Scrod
Cooking tips, 35–37
Corn and crab chowder, 67–68
Court bouillon, 257
Crab:
about, 21
and avocado soup, 58–59
cakes; my own, 214–15
and corn chowder, 67–68
grouper turbans with rémoulade
sauce, 216
in seafood risotto, 97–98
and shrimp with sherry, 213
sole stuffed with, 194

Dip, tuna caper, 50

Escabeche, 41–42

Fish:
about, 5
and beer batter for deep-frying, 259
buying, 7–8
consumption, 6
and cooking methods for, 12–15
cooking times, method of
    determining, 11–12, 37
freezing, 105
and freshness of, 17
frozen, cooking times for, 17
and nutritional information chart on,
    10
raw, 8
stock; white, 258
substitutions, 33–34
and testing for doneness of, 12
and types of, 33–34
see also individual names
Flounder:
about, 21
and carrot-sherry sauce for (variation),
    142
with ginger meunière (substitute), 237
seviche (variation), 49
stuffed with mushrooms with tarragon
    sauce, 177–78
and tarragon sauce for, 249
and tomato-horseradish sauce for, 253
in tomato-mushroom sauce, 131–32
see also Sole

Grilling techniques, 13–14
Grouper:
with anisette and fennel (substitute),
    180
crab turbans with rémoulade sauce,
    216
see also Bass

Haddock:
about, 22
baked, in mornay sauce, 179
broiled, with shrimp-butter sauce
    (substitute), 112
in jalapeño-peanut sauce, 93
Hake with broccoli-cream sauce
    (substitute), 148–49
Halibut:
about, 22
with avocado-cream sauce, 217–18
baked, with carrot and fennel
    (substitute), 199–200
with curry and green chili sauce
    (variation), 111
fillets
    with anisette and fennel, 180

with avocado-cream sauce, 217–18
with broccoli-cream sauce
    (substitute), 148–49
broiled pesto, with another tomato
    sauce, 107
in escabeche, 41–42
provençale (substitute), 157–58
with tomatoes and cucumbers
    (substitute), 105
with ginger meunière (substitute), 237
Moroccan style (substitute), 224–25
and pesto sauce for, 251
and soy marinade for (variation), 240
steaks
    broiled, with sour cream, onions,
        and mushrooms, 106
    with green peppers (substitute), 80
    in sauce piquante, 133–34
    with tomatoes and cucumbers, 105
and tarragon sauce for, 249
in tomato-mushroom sauce
    (substitute), 131–32
Hush puppies, 206–207

The Lancet, 6
Lobster:
about, 22–23
bisque, 60–61
medallions with avocado, mango, and
    basil sauce, 43–44
in seafood risotto, 97–98
Lotte: See Monkfish

Mackerel:
about, 23–24
baked, with three-pepper sauce,
    181–82
broiled, with rhubarb and tomato
    sauce, 110
Mahimahi:
about, 24
in coconut milk, 94–95
with cucumber cream, 135
with mangoes in green peppercorn
    sauce, 219–20
with sun-dried tomatoes and basil
    sauce, 221–22
Microwaving techniques, 14–15
Monkfish:
in a fine kettle o' fish, 70
about, 24
with anisette and fennel (substitute), 180
and leek soup, 62
medallions with tomato-lemon sauce,
    223
with pasta in fresh tomato sauce, 89
with saffron sauce, 136–37

in seafood sausage, 45–46
and shrimp stew, 71
Mussels:
à la marinière, 138
about, 24–25
cleaning, 138
stuffed, 183

National Fisheries Institute, 6, 31
Noodles: See Pasta
Nutritional information chart, 10

Omega 3 fatty acids, 5
Orange roughy:
about, 25
and aioli for, 250
baked, with artichoke-lemon and mint
    sauce, 184
poached, with tomato-butter sauce,
    139
with red pepper sauce, 108
Oysters:
about, 25–26
with orange butter; warm, 54
poached, with cilantro butter,
    mushrooms and bell peppers,
    140–41
Pasta, 87–92
with broccoli and tuna; pesto, 92
fettuccine with white clam sauce,
    87–88
lemon and pepper, sautéed or broiled
    swordfish with (sidebar), 91
linguine
    with monkfish in fresh tomato
        sauce, 89
    with white clam sauce, 87–88
with monkfish in fresh tomato sauce,
    89
noodles and smoked salmon with dill
    sauce, 90
spaghetti with monkfish in fresh
    tomato sauce, 89
squid-ink, with scallops and red
    peppers, 91
with white clam sauce, 87–88
Poaching techniques, 12
Pollock:
about, 26
broiled, with curry and green chile
    sauce, 111
broiled, with shrimp-butter sauce, 112
in tomato-mushroom sauce
    (substitute), 131–32
Pompano:
about, 26
baked, in red wine sauce, 185–86

Prudhomme, Paul, 19, 99
Public Voice for Food and Health
    Policy, 7

Red snapper:
    in a fine kettle o' fish, 70
    about, 26–27
    and aioli for, 250
    baked, with carrot and fennel
        (substitute), 199–200
    baked, with eggplant, basil, and
        coriander, 187–88
    broiled, with shrimp-butter sauce
        (substitute), 112
    in escabeche, 41–42
    Moroccan style, 224–25
    poached, in carrot-sherry sauce,
        142–43
    poached, with crispy shrimp topping,
        144–45
    with sake and black bean sauce, 189
    seviche (variation), 49
    with tomato sauce and bananas,
        226–28
Rémoulade sauce, 254
Risotto, seafood, 97–98
Roe: See Caviar; Salmon roe; Shad roe

Salad(s), 75–83
    catfish-potato, 75
    cooked fish, with carrots and
        tomatoes, 76
    salmon (sidebar), 146
    salmon niçoise, 77–78
    shrimp sunomono (Japanese-style), 79
    swordfish with green peppers, 80
    tuna
        the best, 81
        in coconut milk and lime, 82
        pokee, 83
Salmon:
    about, 27
    fillets
        broiled, with tomato sauce and
            garlic cream, 114–15
        grilled, with leeks and
            tarragon-honey glaze, 116–17
        poached in orange juice and wine,
            147
        poached, with cumin sauce, 146
        in vodka-cream sauce with green
            peppercorns, 229
    niçoise, 77–78
    poached in orange juice and wine,
        147
    salad (sidebar), 146

salad with carrots and tomatoes;
    cooked, 76
smoked
    with dill sauce; noodles and, 90
    and soy marinade for (variation), 240
    steaks with mustard-mint sauce, 113
    tartare (substitute), 51
    in vodka-cream sauce with green
        peppercorns, 229
Sand dabs: See Flounder
Sauce(s), 245–56
    aioli, 250
    apple cream, 55
    artichoke-lemon and mint, 184
    avocado-cream, 217–18
    basil, 43–44
    beurre blanc, 246
    black butter, 153
    brandy and orange, 190
    broccoli-cream, 148–49
    caper-cream, 154
    carrot-sherry, 142–43
    caviar butter, 197
    clam, white, 87–88
    cream, 52–53
    cucumber cream, 135
    cumin, 146
    curry and green chile, 111
    dill, 90
    dill butter, melted, 159
    farmer cheese, yogurt, and mint, 170
    garlic-butter, 230
    green peppercorn, 219–20
    gribiche, 165–66
    herbed butter, 247
    jalapeño-peanut, 93
    lemon-caper, 204
    lemon-ginger, 167–68
    macadamia nut, 195–96
    mornay, 245
    mushroom-watercress, 234–35
    mustard-mint, 113
    mustard-thyme mayonnaise, 231
    orange butter, 54
    papaya, 124–26
    parsley-walnut, 120
    parsley with clams, 150
    pecan butter, 208–10
    pepper, red, 108
    pepper, red and yellow, 122–23
    pesto, 251
    piquante, 133–34
    rémoulade, 254
    rhubarb and tomato, 110
    saffron, 136–37
    sake and black bean, 189
    sesame-orange, 256

shallot-wine, 48
shrimp-butter, 112
sour cream, onions, and mushrooms,
    106
sun-dried tomato butter, 248
sun-dried tomatoes and basil, 221–22
tarragon, 249
tartar, 255
three-pepper, 181–82
tomato, 173, 226–28
tomato, another, 252
tomato-butter, 139
tomato, fresh, 89
tomato, green pepper and basil,
    127–28
tomato-horseradish, 253
tomato-lemon, 223
tomato-mushroom, 131–32
tomato, roasted, 114–15
tomato, spicy, 160
vodka-cream with green peppercorns,
    229
white, basic, 245
white clam, 87–88
wine, red, 185–86
yogurt, spicy, 151–52
Sausage, seafood, 45–46
Sautéing techniques, 13
Scallops:
    about, 27
    bay
        in garlic-butter sauce, 230
        with mustard-thyme mayonnaise,
            231
        and red peppers; squid-in pasta
            with, 91
    and beer batter for deep-frying, 259
    curried, 95–96
    and garlic soup; creamy, 63–64
    with mushroom-watercress sauce
        (substitute), 234–35
    sea
        curried, 95–96
        and garlic soup; creamy, 63–64
        and red peppers; squid-ink pasta
            with, 91
Scrod:
    with broccoli-cream sauce, 148–49
    and carrot-sherry sauce for (variation),
        142
    in parsley sauce with clams, 150
    in spicy yogurt sauce, 151–52
    and tarragon sauce for, 249
    see also Cod
Sea bass: See Bass
Seafood:
    most popular, 31

Seafood (continued)
  risotto, 97–98
  sausage, 45–46
  see also Fish; Shellfish; individual
    names
Shad, 27–28
Shad roe:
  about, 28
  broiled, 118
Shark:
  about, 28
  baked, with carrot and fennel
    (substitute), 199–200
  and pesto sauce for, 251
  with sake and lemon juice, 119
  and soy marinade for (variation), 240
  steaks
    broiled, with green olive tapenade,
      121
    with green peppers (substitute), 80
    with parsley-walnut sauce, 120
    with sake and lemon juice, 119
Shellfish:
  and nutritional information chart on,
    10
  see also individual names
Shrimp:
  about, 28–29
  and beer batter for deep-frying, 259
  butter sauce; broiled pollock with,
    112
  with cabbage and caviar, 161–62
  Cajun style; baked, 99
  celery chowder, 69
  and crab with sherry, 213
  creole, 101–102
  with lime and avocado, 232–33
  and monkfish stew, 71
  with mushroom-watercress sauce,
    234–35
  poached in beer with melted dill
    butter, 159
  with red peppers; Brazilian, 100
  in seafood risotto, 97–98
  in seafood sausage, 45–46
  in spicy tomato sauce, 160
  and striped bass casserole, 198
  sunomono (Japanese-style salad), 79
  topping; poached red snapper with
    crispy, 144–45
Skate:
  about, 29
  with black butter, 153
  poached in sauce gribiche, 165–66
  poached, with cilantro vinaigrette,
    163–64
Smoked trout: *See* Trout

Snapper, red: *See* Red snapper
Sole:
  and carrot-sherry sauce for (variation),
    142
  gray, with ginger meunière
    (substitute), 237
  with lemon-ginger sauce and fried
    leeks, 167–68
  lemon, with ginger meunière, 237
  with macadamia nut sauce, 195–96
  meunière; classic, 236
  piccata with sherry and capers,
    238–39
  stuffed with crabmeat, 194
  and tarragon sauce for, 249
  see also Flounder
Soup(s), 56–69
  chowders
    clam, my favorite, 65–66
    crab and corn, 67–68
    shrimp-celery, 69
  clam and fennel, 56–57
  clam chowder, my favorite, 65–66
  crab and avocado, 58–59
  crab and corn chowder, 67–68
  leek and monkfish, 62
  lobster bisque, 60–61
  scallop and garlic, creamy, 63–64
  shrimp-celery chowder, 69
  see also Stew; Stock
Spaghetti: *See* Pasta
Squid:
  and beer batter for deep-frying, 259
Squid-ink pasta: *See* Pasta
Steaming techniques, 14
Stew:
  fish, a fine kettle o', 70
  monkfish and shrimp, 71
  tuna, Indonesian, 72
Stock:
  court bouillon, 257
  white fish, 258
Striped bass: *See* Bass
Swordfish:
  about, 29–30
  with green peppers, 80
  and pesto sauce for, 251
  sautéed or broiled, with lemon and
    pepper pasta (sidebar), 91
  steaks
    baked, with carrot and fennel,
      199–200
    with green peppers, 80
    grilled, with papaya sauce, 124–26
    with red and yellow pepper sauces,
      122–23
    sautéed, in soy marinade, 240

Tartar sauce, 255
Tilefish:
  in a fine kettle o' fish, 70
  about, 30
  and aioli for, 250
  baked, with filberts and cheddar,
    201
  slices; sesame, 241
Trout:
  about, 30
  amandine, 242
  with apple cream sauce, 55
  rainbow, with apple cream sauce, 55
  smoked, and horseradish with
    avocado, 47
Tuna:
  about, 31
  canned
    about, 31
    niçoise (substitute), 77–78
    pesto pasta with broccoli and, 92
    salad; the best, 81
  caper dip with crudités, 50
  in coconut milk and lime, 82
  fillets
    caper dip with crudités, 50
    in escabeche, 41–42
  with forty garlic cloves, 169
  niçoise (substitute), 77–78
  pokee, 83
  salad; the best, 81
  salad with carrots and tomatoes;
    grilled (substitute), 76
  and soy marinade for (variation),
    240
  steaks
    in coconut milk and lime, 82
    with forty garlic cloves, 169
    tartare, 51
    with tomato, green pepper and basil
      sauce, 127–28
  stew; Indonesian, 72
  tartare, 51
  with tomato, green pepper and basil
    sauce, 127–28

White fish stock, 258
White sauce, basic, 245
Whitefish:
  about, 31–32
  and aioli for, 250
  and carrot-sherry sauce for (variation),
    142
  grilled, with marinated peppers and
    tomatillos, 129–30
  in tomato-mushroom sauce
    (substitute), 131–32